TH

THE TUESDAY DOG

JACK STONELEY

TARGET

published by
the Paperback Division of
W. H. Allen & Co. Ltd

A Target Book

Published in 1978
by the Paperback Division of W. H. Allen & Co. Ltd
A Howard & Wyndham Company
44 Hill Street, London W1X 8LB

Printed in Great Britain by
Richard Clay (The Chaucer Press) Ltd, Bungay, Suffolk

ISBN 0 426 20038 1

1

The whimper came from a cubby-hole under the stairs. . .wistful as the cold November wind that swept along the empty lobby making flakes of paint flutter like little pink butterflies on the peeling walls.

The small brown and white bitch was restless — shifting her cumbersome body this way and that as she clawed the damp wooden floorboards. She knew it was nearly time.

The snow-flecked wind grew more ill-tempered now, buffeting the deserted house until it seemed to creak and groan in despair. The bitch cowered as crumbling plaster dappled her soft fur. She shook it off and settled back against the wall, remembering how things used to be.

She remembered when the house was a living thing filled with cosy sounds and familiar smells. A wonderful place to have had her pups. She remembered the blissful evenings slumped across the hearth, blinking into the sunset of the parlour fire and listening to its embers rustle in tiny landslides of glowing ash.

Her wet nose twitched at thoughts of the steamy, stone-flagged scullery bursting with aromas so rich and appetising that, at this moment, even a whiff of them would have seemed as good as a meal. Now there was nothing but the musty smell of emptiness and neglect, and the dust was everywhere except inside her round earthenware feeding dish that shone with unrewarding licks.

She cocked her tousled head and listened in vain for the sounds she knew so well. The reassuring footsteps of the old man. The whispering skirt of the woman who fed her. And the cries of the neighbourhood children from the cobbled street outside. But she heard none of these. Just the wind tormenting the fraying edges of the derelict building and, in the brief lulls, mice pattering across the floorboards like raindrops.

It was two weeks ago when things began to change. The day the monsters came. They roamed the far end of the street crunching everything aside in their relentless path. Brick walls collapsed like tin cans at a fairground, thundering to the ground in great clouds of choking dust.

The terrified bitch had watched it all — cringing in the shadows as the monsters devoured the street bit by bit, scooping up mountains of rubble into their enormous metal jaws as easily as she could have eaten a handful of dog biscuits. All the time getting closer and closer to her own precious doorstep.

It went on for a week. Then there was peace again. But the invaders stayed, gaunt and menacing a few yards away as though resting before the next fearful onslaught.

That same week the children disappeared. It was all very sudden. One day they were there as usual enticing her to sit up for sweets, shaking with laughter when, heavy with her unborn pups, she overbalanced and rolled over onto her back. The next day they were gone. Perhaps the monsters had eaten them too.

Soon after this the bewildered little bitch found herself being brushed aside as men in clomping hob-nailed boots marched in and out of the rooms carrying away the tables, the chairs, the beds — everything, until the place she loved was just an empty shell.

And then came the worst moment of all. The old man looped a length of thin rope round her neck and tied the end to a drainpipe in the yard at the back of the house, telling her to 'stay there old girl.' The woman put a tin plate of meat at the dog's feet. She was crying when the man shouted from the house, urging her to hurry. But she hung back saying at last: 'It seems so heartless leaving the poor thing here like this.'

'We must,' he insisted, 'It's the only way.'

'But what if the lady doesn't come?'

'She will,' he assured her impatiently. 'She's visiting her sister in London. She'll definitely be back this afternoon. She told you herself she'd come straight here and pick the dog up. It'll get a good home. Don't worry — nothing can happen to it for a few hours.'

She still hesitated, ruffling the bitch's throat with the back of her hand. 'Can't we take her with us?' He cursed softly. 'We've been through all that a dozen times. You know very well we can't. You know the council won't allow dogs in the new flat. They'd have us thrown out.'

'Couldn't I wait here until the lady comes, just to make sure everything's all right?' The man shook his head and ushered her away. 'Now come on — we must be off. The taxi's waiting.'

The bitch watched them disappear into the house and heard the front door slam. A few seconds later the purring of the taxi faded and there was a silence such as she had never known before.

Her first reaction was to bound towards the house but she somersaulted as the rope jerked her back, leaving her sprawled on the ground panting with shock. She tried again and again, each time coughing and spluttering as the noose dug more viciously into her soft throat. She drew back, thrusting against her front legs until her claws grated painfully across the flagstone. But the rope held and, at last, exhausted and confused, she flopped down with her chin between her paws and howled.

Every instinct still urged her to find some way of getting back into the house. Perhaps the man and the woman were still there. She sniffed the other end of the rope. It was firmly knotted to the drainpipe. There seemed only one other thing she could do. She lay down again, gathered the rope in her mouth and chewed and chewed and chewed until her jaws ached. She must have gnawed away for more than an hour. But it worked. One by one the fibres snapped until, suddenly with a mighty tug, she was free.

She scratched the back door and barked. It was a piercing desperate bark. Anyone inside would have had to be stone deaf not to hear it. But, when she pricked her ears, there were no footsteps and no voices. Nothing but the irregular tip-tapping from the first raindrops of an approaching storm against the scullery window. The bitch spun round and ran through the open backyard gate and along the narrow passage at the side of the house leading into the street. The monsters were still there, guarding misshapen monuments of rubble that had once been cosy little homes . . . poised like vultures over half-eaten prey. Nothing stirred and everywhere was as silent as a graveyard.

The bitch ducked as the black sky growled like a wild beast and spat into her face making her screw up her small eyes. She scraped furiously at her front door. An enormous clap of thunder made her almost jump out of her shaggy fur coat and she scampered back along the passage into the yard. The rain was lashing the flagstones now with terrifying fury. For a few moments the bitch huddled against the back door then, glancing up into the rain, she noticed the latticed scullery window was not quite closed. A metal dustbin stood directly beneath it. In a flash she leapt onto it and stretched herself against the wall. An instant later she was squirming through the gap and crashing unladylike onto her back in the big scullery sink. She shook herself vigorously and vaulted over the edge onto the floor.

For a while she stood there, rock-still, urging her keen doggy senses to the limit. Then she darted from room to room, her long ragged tail drooping lower and lower. They were all the same. Like big empty boxes. She was about to rush up the steep narrow staircase in the lobby but drew back. The rooms above were not for dogs. The foot of the stairs was a frontier the woman had taught her never to cross and, even now, desperate though she was, the little dog did not dare to step beyond it. Instead she listened and sniffed and knew there was no one up there anyway. Feeling confused and betrayed she curled up in what seemed to her the safest place — the tiny cubby-hole behind the door under the stairs.

It was some hours later that a woman peered over the backyard wall and saw a piece of chewed-up rope dangling from the drainpipe. She sighed. 'The poor thing's broken loose,' she told herself. The woman called and called the dog's name, but the wind snatched her voice away each time. She didn't notice the partly-opened scullery window so she ran along the cobbled passage glancing through each unlocked yard door. 'It could be miles away by now,' she muttered, flicking rat-tails of dripping hair from her face. Finally, she shook her head, clicked her tongue, and hurried off in the rain.

2

The lonely little bitch scratched feverishly at a crumpled heap of old newspapers she had dragged into her cubby-hole from the litter-strewn lobby. She sensed that very soon more than merely her own survival would be at stake.

Since the man and the woman left five days ago, her only concern had been finding enough food to keep herself alive. Most of it she had scavenged from the overflow of waste bins in nearby occupied streets, leaving and entering her own house through the scullery window. There had never been any question of her seeking a new home. The man and the woman would come back. She was sure of that.

She closed her eyes and arched her back against the cubby-hole wall. The muscles in her body began to tense and relax . . . tense and relax . . . in the first gentle rhythm of birth. Soon the straining became more rapid — urging, coaxing, hurrying along the tiny creatures huddled up inside her. Letting her know it was time. Time for them to face a not very inviting world.

Suddenly the first pup arrived — soft and sleeky and seemingly gift-wrapped in a thin silky membrane sack. Instinctively, the bitch tore it apart and licked the puppy vigorously, rolling it over onto its back. It was a black and white bitch.

Next her sharp teeth nipped through the slender umbilical cord close to the puppy's stomach, casting it adrift from her own body for the first time. And there it lay, warm and wet with tight little eyes and crumpled ears and legs that seemed utterly inadequate. The bitch rustled alongside it on the bed of newspapers and the pup nuzzled sightlessly towards its mother's teats. Within minutes the bitch was spurring on the next of her litter.

It was two hours later that the third and final pup emerged. The bitch was very tired now, but she felt happy and contented. Even her ordeals of the last few days were forgotten. As the wind hummed a lullaby through the empty house, she curled about her babies and slept. It had been a long hard day for them all. But now at least she wasn't lonely any more.

It is indeed remarkable that there were still three puppies grimly holding on to their brand new lives the next morning. Probably it was the snow that saved them. It had tumbled down in great fluffy chunks, insulating the whole house — tucking it in for the night beneath a blanket thicker than lambswool. Soft white dunes of it had clawed halfway up the front door and sealed the gaps in the ill-fitting window frames until the wind had given up trying to get in and had dozed off too.

Now, as the winter sun came streaming into the parlour, the bitch tenderly picked up each pup by the scruff of its neck and laid them under the window to bask in the glow. The instant she stretched out beside them they clung to her like leeches, burrowing into her warm fur in a frantic free-for-all to claim their share of nourishment.

They were a motley little family sucking away there in the sunlight. Already, though only twelve hours old, the first-born — the black and white bitch — had established its seniority by barging through the others to the warmest spot under its mother's hind leg. Here too, the milk was more abundant. The two male pups — one fawn, the other jet black, were too small and feeble to object.

It is extremely doubtful if a large litter could have survived that first night. However, as things had worked out, there was plenty for all and nipples to spare. But for how long? The bitch raised her head and winced as the largest offspring thrust its front paws against her milk glands to urge on its own personal supply. It was obvious that if any of the pups were to stay alive for long, she herself would have to find food. Without it there could be no milk. And getting it meant leaving them alone in the house . . . something opposed to all her instincts as a mother. They had to be constantly loved and licked and kept warm.

She stayed with them all that day. Fortunately, the weather remained mild, easing the snow's grip on the roof until it slid gracefully over the edges making noises like the wind, and pounded into slushy heaps on the flagstones below. And all that night her body hugged away the cold as they slept. Next morning, however, the urgent rumble of her stomach convinced her that food must be her first concern, outweighing any perils the pups might face during the short time she would be away seeking it.

By midday it was quite warm. This was the time to go. The bitch carried fresh newspaper from the lobby and arranged the twitching pups close together. Then, after licking each in turn, she backed out of the cubby-hole, drawing closed the door with her front paw. She bounded across the scullery, launching herself into the air and hooking her front legs over the edge of the sink, scrabbling with her back ones until she toppled inside. Here she hesitated, ears alert, staring ruefully back along the lobby. A moment later she was through the window and on her way.

She trotted purposefully from street to street, head high and nostrils tweaking, sifting the most promising odours from the breeze; stopping occasionally and stretching up on short hind legs to nudge aside a dustbin lid. She sensed nothing edible, which wasn't surprising as a garbage man had already toured the district and taken the lot.

An hour later she was desperate. She had already been away from her pups too long. Turning off into a narrow lane she found herself in a large open yard. Ahead was a brick building and despite the weather a group of men squatted on wooden boxes in a doorway. The bitch watched them for a while. They were eating from paper bags. She flattened against the ground and moved closer tilting her head from side to side.

'Here fella . . . here fella!' The bitch stiffened and backed away. The man's voice *seemed* friendly enough but she wasn't sure. 'C'mon then . . . c'mon boy,' it coaxed. She half turned to run, but the thought of her hungry pups stopped her. The man had food. Food necessary for her to make milk. Whether he was friendly or not she had to take a chance. She crouched again and crept towards him. As she did so, he delved into his paper bag and held something at arm's length. 'Hungry?' he whispered. The bitch panted, sniffed a few times, then whipped away the morsel as cleanly as a seagull sweeping up flotsam, gulping it down in one piece. The man blew on his fingers and grinned at the others. He waited until the dog edged forward again then slid a chunk of meat from between two slices of bread. As she was about to snap at it, he lifted it out of reach. 'Wait for it, fella,' he chided. 'Take it easy. Where're your manners?' He lowered it again. 'Gently . . .' She gripped the meat gingerly between her teeth and slowly drew it away. 'That's better,' he smiled. 'Friends now, are we?'

She didn't flinch when he ruffled her ear. In fact she grew even bolder and nudged the paper bag with her nose. The man chuckled and shook out the rest of the contents. 'Cheeky monkey . . . here, help yourself.' He didn't have to invite her twice. She swept up every scrap with the efficiency of a vacuum cleaner.

Still hungry, however, she moved to the next man and laid her chin on his knee, eyeing his paper bag with such dolefulness that he too emptied it before her. 'There, you scraggy little thing,' he grunted good-naturedly. 'Now are you satisfied?' Normally she might have been. But there were three other stomachs to be filled now — stomachs that would demand more every day. So she continued her head-on-lap routine until she couldn't eat another thing.

As she stood there panting her gratitude, a deafening high-pitched wail sent her skidding behind one of the wooden boxes. Everyone roared with laughter and the first man knelt down and stroked the fur that prickled in fright along her back. 'It's all right fella, it's all right,' he consoled her. 'It's only the factory hooter. But that's it for now, I'm afraid. We've got work to do.'

As the men wandered off the little dog wagged her tail. They hadn't seen the last of her.

It was much colder as she headed for home, carefully noting the route. An icy wind rampaged through the maze of streets, bullying her at every turn. One mighty blow bowled her over into a shop doorway. She lay panting for a while then, remembering her pups, lowered her head and pushed on defiantly.

Ten minutes later she was leaping onto the dustbin in her own backyard and squeezing under the scullery window. She scampered along the lobby then stopped and pricked her ears outside the cubby-hole door. There was a faint rustle of newspapers. She wasn't too late after all.

Bursting with joy she thumped open the door and lay beside her pups, stretching and turning for them to suckle. She felt the warm, eager tongue of the bitch as it scrambled into its usual spot under her hind leg. Then she sensed the more feeble efforts of another. She waited. But that was all she felt. She raised her head. One puppy wasn't feeding — the black one. She licked it but it didn't respond.

Without fuss, after the other two had stopped feeding, the bitch rucked its soft skin between her teeth and carried it across the lobby and into the parlour. Here, in a corner of the empty room, she laid it down very gently. She stood looking at it, her head cocked to one side. And then, a moment later, she turned and walked away.

3

During the next forty-eight hours the bitch was reluctant to leave her two remaining pups for a moment. Though ravenously hungry, she had not dared to risk another journey for food.

But the fawn one was getting weaker. Its breathing was barely discernible when it lay at her side. The other was active enough — guzzling her for all it was worth and obviously determined to survive. But what milk there was left gave little nourishment. The bitch knew she had to leave them again. It seemed doubtful the feebler pup could hold on until she returned, but at least the other might still have a chance. Before she left she covered them both with every newspaper she could find.

She first considered foraging close to the house hoping for something to turn up. But what if nothing did? She had to find food that day. Tomorrow could be too late. Instead she decided to head straight for the factory. It was a long way but at least she was reasonably sure of some wholesome food. That was most important. Scraps weren't enough to make good rich milk.

She tore off at full speed. Apart from a few indecisive pauses she remembered the way well enough and, twenty minutes later, was turning into the narrow lane panting in expectation. She was sure this was the place. There was the brick building. There were the wooden boxes. *But where were the men with the paper bags?* Her tail drooped. They had to be here, but the yard was empty.

She was about to turn back when that ear-rending wailing sound she'd heard before made her jerk with fright. A moment later she was hurtling across the yard barking and lashing her tail. As the man striding out of the door spread his arms, she took a flying leap, thumping into his chest and almost bowling him off his feet.

'What the blazes . . .' he puffed, hanging on to her as she lapped his face. He held her aloft in his powerful hands and laughed loudly. 'Oh, so it's you is it?' He glanced back. 'Hey Stan, look who's come to see us. Hope you've brought plenty of grub.' The other slapped his forehead. 'Oh no!' he groaned. 'I'm starving, and the wife's made my favourite sandwiches . . . roast pork and onion. That little terror's got an appetite like a goat.'

Two other men came out and all four sat on the wooden boxes. And — joy of joys — they'd all brought their paper bags! The bitch's eyes glowed as the men fussed her. But she was impatient to get started. There was no time for frivolities. She knew she had to eat up and get home as quickly as possible. She prodded the nearest bag and barked. The man shook his head. 'Well now, we are in a hurry, aren't we,' he smiled. 'D'you mind if I join you? After all it is my lunch.'

The bitch anxiously trod the ground. If only he realised it was a matter of life and death. But how could he? And how could she tell him? She lay down, realising she would just have to be patient.

Fortunately, they didn't keep her waiting long. Her pitiful expression was too much to ignore. After a few mouthfuls they were handing out their food as rapidly as she could swallow it. Once full she was on her way. 'There's gratitude for you,' muttered Stan. 'Cupboard love, that's all it is.' The first man watched her disappear along the lane and frowned. 'I wonder,' he said, '. . . I wonder. He's an intelligent little chap that one. Somehow I had the feeling he was trying to tell us something.' The other shrugged. 'Maybe you're right.' Then he grinned and added: 'By the way he's not a chap — he's a girl.'

'Oh is he? You know, I never noticed.'

Fuelled by a full stomach, the bitch raced home in record time, but, for the fawn pup even that wasn't fast enough. By the time its mother arrived there was only one mouth to feed in the cubby-hole under the stairs. . .

There were to be no further visits to the factory. Instead the bitch, determined to preserve her last pup, confined her search for food to the immediate neighbourhood. It meant having to make three or four rapid tours a day, but this way the pup was never left alone for very long. The rest of the time the devoted mother rarely let the pup out of her sight, lavishing affection and carrying it about with her wherever she went.

The situation was desperate for a while. The bitch hardly found enough scraps to stay alive herself. But the pup was a sturdy, tenacious creature and stubbornly refused to leave the world without a fight. So, somehow, they hung on together until, after a week, things began to improve. The bitch found a number of life-savers. An old woman three streets away left cat meat on her garden wall . . . easily reachable from the top of a dustbin unless the bad-tempered cat got to it first. A group of children began sharing their packed lunches with her on their way to school. She also mastered the art of dragging bottles of milk from doorsteps and piercing the tops with her teeth. The weather, too, improved and she found a thick woollen jersey looped over a rope in someone's yard and furnished the cubby-hole with it. All in all the future appeared to be far less grim.

Some truly remarkable things were now happening to the fumbling little puppy bitch. To start with, the world changed from black to grey and became filled with blurred shapes. Very soon these grew crystal clear so that she no longer had to grope blindly about the house. She suddenly found she could raise herself off the ground—only for a second, mind you, until her feet splayed out and down she would crash onto her belly. But she soon got used to the idea and eventually was able to move herself from place to place.

Another thing she noticed was that the world wasn't silent any more. The newspaper crackled when she rolled on it; doors creaked in the wind and even her own paws chattered softly to her as they shuffled about the house. Her mother seemed to know what it all meant and frequently licked her milky-blue eyes and washed out her ears.

In fact there was something new and wonderful happening all the time. Now, when her mother went off for food, there was plenty to do and each day she became more adventurous, sniffing in corners and sneezing the dust from her nose. She sought out tiny creatures with legs no thicker than a strand of her own fur that raced up walls when she nudged them.

She screwed up her new eyes and yapped at the dazzling shafts of winter sunlight streaking through the parlour window as swirling clouds of dust made them appear to move and breathe like living things. She even tried climbing the stairs in the lobby until her mother dragged her back by the scruff of her neck and shook her firmly. The pup, too, had to learn she couldn't go up there.

The pup was five weeks old when the sleeping monsters outside stirred again and yawned their great metal jaws. The bitch heard them and bustled her inquisitive offspring from the parlour into the cubby-hole where she gripped the door-latch with her teeth and heaved it shut. A few moments later she heard muffled voices and the door at the end of the lobby burst open. The floor shuddered as heavy footsteps pounded passed her hideaway. The voices were loud now, echoing through the bare rooms.

'Right then . . . Jim, Ken — you start inside. Clear out the decent timber. Leave the rest. It'll burn. I'll make a start on the roof.'

The bitch pricked her ears as more crunching footsteps thudded up the staircase above her head, shaking down a shower of plaster that sent the pup scurrying into a corner. Then the most fearsome things began to happen. It seemed as if the whole building was about to tear itself apart as it groaned and trembled. The bitch slipped a paw round the cubby-hole door and looked out. A terrifying roar made her leap back. A deafening avalanche of bricks and timber crashed into the lobby. The bitch curled round the pup, which was staring up at her wide-eyed and no doubt wondering why it had struggled so hard to stay in such a frightening world.

The turmoil lasted most of the morning. Then the dogs heard the front door slam and the workmen's footsteps trail away down the street. The bitch waited a moment then ventured timidly into the lobby. It was like a battlefield with broken bricks and ragged pieces of timber heaped about the floor. She listened carefully. Everywhere was quiet apart from the occasional trickle of plaster from the rooms above. The bitch crossed the lobby into the parlour. The walls were still standing, but she trembled violently because she was sure they would come down soon . . . and she and her pup had to get away before they did.

She now noticed an odd thing. She was certain it was still early in the day, yet the room was in darkness. No light came from the window except through small chinks in wooden boards that had been fixed across it from the outside. There was something else, too. The smell; sharp and pungent like the stuff the woman used to pour onto wood in the firegrate before setting it alight. Then she saw the smoke, gliding like a ghost from a pile of rags and timber in the furthest corner of the room. It thickened, stinging her eyes and catching her throat. She raced into the scullery and froze. The partly-opened window she'd been using was boarded up too . . . and there was no other way out.

She hurried back to the parlour. A bright orange tongue of flame danced over the smouldering rubbish and the smoke curled out along the lobby. A frantic yelping sent her rushing back to the cubby-hole. She dragged the pup into the scullery then threw herself at the back door, gouging splinters of wood with her claws and howling as she had never howled before.

She hauled the pup back along the lobby, tumbling over the rubble until she reached the front door. As she passed the parlour she could see the restless flames creeping along the floor and licking the walls. A gust of heat made her gasp. She leapt and crashed her body hard against the door time and again until she dropped exhausted, coughing smoke from her aching lungs.

There was only one other way to go and that was up the stairs. The pup was already trying to heave its squirming body over the bottom one. Instinctively the bitch held it back and growled. Even now she could not bring herself to cross that forbidden frontier. The pup again attempted to clamber up, nipping and snarling as its mother barred the way. The bitch glanced across the lobby. A sharp burst of flame whiplashed round the parlour door. She looked back at the stairs. Surely the woman would understand — just this once. She snatched the pup and scrambled up.

Dropping the pup on the landing, she roamed the empty rooms, sniffing the skirting boards, her tail curled between her legs in fear. She sprang at the window sills, hanging from them until her claws made deep furrows in the wood. But the windows were closed tight. They were still trapped, and there were no more stairs.

She tore madly from room to room again, desperately searching for a way out. Grey smoke spattered with floating ash rose from the rooms below and the flickering glow on the staircase wall told her the flames were not far behind. She dragged the whimpering pup into the nearest room and lay close to her, sensing death.

It was then she saw the hole in the wall. The

one with the small tiled arch above. It was like the larger one downstairs where she had spent so many cosy hours. She sniffed around it — instinctively drawing back, remembering how the blazing embers used to spit at her when the woman stirred it to life with her shiny brass rod. But this one was dead and empty. There was nothing to fear, cold air greeted her nostrils and she guessed this was the way out. She moved closer and looked up to find herself peering into the mouth of a tunnel. Thrusting her front paws inside, she reared up onto her hind legs. It was pitch dark and her eyes narrowed as soot showered down like black snow.

She shook herself and dropped back on all fours. As smoke snaked into the room from the landing the choking pup nuzzled between her legs as if urging her on. The bitch still hesitated, but she knew it was either the black hole or the hungry flames now crackling along the banister rail.

The way in through the dark throat of the tunnel was narrow — a gap no wider than her own body, but the few feet she could discern beyond was broader and seemed to lead off at an angle. Once through the gap she felt certain she could scramble further.

She bit into the back of the pup's neck and heaved it above her head, ramming the infant and the top part of her own body through the gap, hind legs scrabbling wildly for paw-holds to force the rest of herself through. She found a footing and strained hard, battling to keep a hold on the pup and scraping up the tunnel wall with her front claws. But she couldn't move any further. Her body was wedged tight, as though the jaws of the tunnel were closing in on her.

The pup had slipped from her mouth and lay

helpless on its back between her paws. She allowed her body to relax for a moment. Both hind feet then found a firmer hold and, summing up every ounce of strength, the determined bitch made a final lunge. The vice-like grip round her middle eased and she was through the gap, licking her pup's face and spitting out the soot.

After a short rest the bitch picked up the pup again and began the tortuous ascent. There were plenty of paw-holds now. Bricks jutted from the sides of the tunnel and, as she'd noticed earlier, its course was steep but not vertical. There was more room too, which provided better leverage as she groped and heaved her way up, cradling the pup between her front legs whenever she paused for breath.

Then suddenly the route changed. It didn't slope any more. It went straight up. The bitch wedged herself across the tunnel and sniffed the inky blackness ahead. Somewhere up there was a way out. She could sense it. Somewhere up there was fresh, clean air. But how far? And how could she possibly climb a vertical shaft with a puppy in her mouth?

A waft of searing heat swept from the room below. The tunnel was filling with smoke. She knew she had to go on or die, entombed where they were. A mouse scurried past them and on into oblivion. If only they could climb as easily as that.

The bitch took a firm grip on the pup's neck and probed blindly for footholds with her front paws. Then, with a tremendous thrust of thighs she powered herself upwards. All four legs now pummelled, scraped and clawed frenziedly against the tunnel sides as, inch by inch, she began to urge her body on . . . driving every muscle until they seemed they must tear apart. Inch by gruelling inch . . . ripping her paws on barnacles of mortar, her lungs bursting for air. The pup too seemed to sense what they had to do and started scratching like a mole. Inch by agonising inch . . . the bitch writhed, twisted and flexed her small body, wildly frisking the rough tunnel wall with her legs for more footholds as a knife-edge of brick tore a gash in her side. Her jaws ached from the weight of the pup.

If the vertical section of the tunnel had not changed course at that moment, the struggle would have been over. The bitch knew there was no way she could have carried on. But it *did* change. It began to slope again.

She collapsed against the wall, wheezing in pain. The pup now lay limp between her paws. She licked it furiously. She couldn't let it die now . . . not after all this.

Eyes closed and every muscle throbbing for mercy, she dragged the pup on up the slope. She became aware of the torn flesh in her side and wanted to lick it but feared that if she released the pup she might not have the strength to gather it up again. Now every movement sent blood pounding into her ears and, when she thrust forward, her back legs doubled up beneath her. She had nothing more to give. With a deep sigh her jaw sagged and the pup rolled under her throat and lay still . . .

. . . Then, quite suddenly, a bird cheeped. The bitch looked up and saw the sky. And there, peering in at her was a sparrow, tilting its head and wondering why on earth a couple of dogs were nesting in a chimney stack.

4

"Hey Ken — look! There. . .on the roof!'

'Crikey, I don't believe it. It's a dog!'

'And a pup. See it?'

'Well I'll be . . . how the devil did they get up there?'

'The chimney. The one we started knocking down this morning. It's incredible — they've climbed the chimney. They must have.'

'Well for Pete's sake, let's do something.'

'What about the fire brigade?'

'No time. The poor things will be roasted alive.'

The man swung round and pointed to the great steel excavator parked across the street. 'We'll use that, Jim — come on.' He dragged the other towards it and pushed him into the square cab mounted on caterpillar tracks. 'Right,' he yelled, 'lower the jib.'

As the machine shuddered to life with a roar and a grinding of gears, its gigantic arm bent at the elbow until the serrated jaw of the heavy metal scoop touched the ground. 'That's it. Now, I'll get in here.' He stepped inside and crouched down, gripping the top edge. 'Right,' he bawled at the top of his voice, jabbing a finger towards the roof, 'up we go!' The long jib tilted and straightened out lifting the scoop high into the air.

The bitch, more dead than alive and black as a raven,

lay panting over the apex of the roof, her pup gripped between blood-stained teeth. The final foot or so up the chimney stack and onto the roof had sapped away her last dregs of energy. She heard the men shouting in the street. They must have seen her. She had to hang on for the pup's sake. No — it wasn't dead. In fact once it had gulped fresh air into its hungry lungs, the rugged little creature began yelping and squirming as the bitch held grimly on, her jaws feeling as if they must snap at any moment.

Suddenly, through glazed eyes, she saw the monster looming over the edge of the roof, its mouth sagging wide. She backed away in horror.

It was only a few feet away now, its long neck swaying like a cobra. The pup saw it too. It curled up and, with a sudden thrust of its back legs, twisted from its mother's grip. The bitch lurched to retrieve it but was too late. The pup, yelping in terror, its tiny legs splayed out, slid backwards on its stomach, vainly trying to gain a hold on the wet grey slates with its paws.

'The pup!' screamed a woman in the street covering her eyes. 'It's dropped the pup!' The man in the monster's jaws froze as the helpless animal slithered on towards the edge of the roof. He leaned out as far as he dared and stretched his arm. The pup slipped past, only inches from his fingertips. 'Poor little wretch,' he groaned, gritting his teeth and listening for the inevitable crunch of its soft body against the pavement. But there wasn't one. He glanced down. Miraculously its hind feet had wedged themselves in an open drainpipe running along the edge of the roof and it lay there pressed flat against the slates.

The man in the cab saw it and was already backing

up the machine and lowering the jib towards the trembling pup. An instant later the other man was gathering it up in his huge hand and hugging it to his chest. 'There,' he whispered, '. . .now let's sort out your mum.' He gave a thumbs up sign and the scoop reared again, easing forward towards the bitch. As it hovered a couple of feet away the man stuffed the pup into his overall top leaving both arms free, which he held out inviting the bitch to leap into them. Instead she arched her back and snarled. She wasn't going to give in to the monster without a fight. 'What's the matter old girl?' coaxed the man patting his knee. 'Come on then. You can make it.'

The woman in the street screamed again as a bedroom window shattered and a shaft of orange flame burst through, curling its way up the roof. Smoke too was now surging between the slates making the man heave and cough. 'For pity's sake,' he yelled, '. . .jump!' The bitch stared wide-eyed into the flame and her muscles locked in fright.

Very gently the man in the cab fractionally moved a lever at his side. The scoop glided forward those vital inches. Before the bitch could dodge away, her front legs were gripped tight. She struggled but, a second later, was firmly tucked under the other man's arm. The monster half pirouetted and lowered its head smoothly to the ground.

The man climbed out of the scoop as his colleague hurried across and fondled the bitch's muzzle. She made a feeble effort to lick him then wearily flopped her chin into the palm of his hand instead and closed her eyes. 'She's all in Ken,' he said softly, 'D'you think they'll be all right?' He lifted one of her legs and shook his head. 'Look at these paws — they're raw.'

The other man stroked her side and stared at his fingers. 'She's bleeding too. Must have ripped herself on something.' He winced and glanced down at the pup inside his overalls. 'Ouch . . . this little chap seems lively enough. It's nibbling me.'

'What do we do with them now?'

'Don't know.'

'Suppose we ought to take them to the police or something.'

'Suppose so, Jim.' The bitch was now fast asleep, her chin draped over the man's forearm. The pup squeezed its head between the overall buttons and started licking its mother's ear. 'Yes, you might well do that little 'un,' the man smiled. 'She's certainly saved your skin today.' He carefully turned his wrist trying not to disturb the sleeping bitch. 'Look Jim, it's nearly lunch-time. Suppose I take them home. The wife's a dab hand with animals. She'll know what to do.' The other beamed. 'I was hoping you'd say that.'

His colleague frowned. 'We couldn't keep 'em of course.'

'No, 'course you couldn't, Ken.'

'I mean we haven't got the room.'

''Course you haven't, Ken.'

'I'll be back in an hour.'

Ken Taylor's wife was a pink-faced, roly-poly woman, soft and dumpy like the great mound of pastry she was about to flatten under her rolling pin when her husband tapped the back door with the toe of his boot. 'Who's that?' she called dusting the flour from her hands.

'It's me . . . Ken.'

'Ken — at this time?' she muttered opening the door. 'You've not been sacked have you? It's only . . . good grief, Ken! What on earth's that!'

She threw up her chubby hands and stared at the bedraggled bitch drooped over his arms. Then she threw them up again when a small grubby face emerged from her husband's overalls. 'Oh the poor things . . . the poor, poor things. What happened? Have they been run over?' She bustled him into the kitchen. 'No love,' he said, '. . . they've been up a chimney.'

'Up a chimney!'

She delved inside his overalls and lifted out the sooty pup, cuddling it like a baby until her rosy cheeks turned black too. 'B-but why? Where? I don't understand, Ken.'

He moved into the living-room and lowered himself into the sofa by the fire, the lifeless bitch still in his arms. 'It was at that slum clearance site we've been working on. You know the one.' She followed him, anxiously perching on the edge of the sofa as the pup chewed her meaty finger. Then she gently brushed the fur along the side of the older dog's body. 'Oh Ken, look . . . it's been injured.'

'Yes, I know.'

The woman moved rapidly, yet with the calm assurance of someone who could always be relied upon to do the right thing at the right time. She clattered about the kitchen, returning with a bowl of steaming water in one hand and lint, cotton wool, bandages and safety pins in the other. A thick woolly blanket was over her right arm and a bottle of milk under her left. They all tumbled about her as she came to roost again on the sofa. 'Ooh, it's nasty,' she cringed, soaking the lint and dabbing it along the dog's wound.

'Reckon she ripped herself on something in that chimney.'

'But, Ken — how in heaven's name did she climb it. . .and with a puppy? I mean just look at it — it can't be more than a few weeks old.'

'Don't ask me how, Alice. But it did. And if that isn't motherly devotion for you, I don't know what is. I reckon that little 'un's a real fighter too. It doesn't seem any the worse now, does it?' As if to confirm this, the pup rolled over and curled itself round the woman's hand, pummelling it with its short back legs. 'Here, Ken,' she ordered, 'give the mite some of this. It must be starved.' She passed him the bottle of milk. He fetched a saucer from the kitchen and filled it to the brim, watching incredulously as the pup's pink tongue fluttered through it like a tiny outboard motor. His wife patted her eyes with the hem of her apron. 'Bless it,' she snivelled, carrying on bathing the bitch. 'I do hope its mother will be all right.'

'I think the poor thing's exhausted, that's all,' assured her husband.

'I'm not surprised. It's amazing she's still alive.' She laid a dry piece of lint over the dog's side. 'The wound isn't as deep as I thought, Ken. It's rest she needs. Lots of rest.' She spread the blanket before the fire. 'Bring her over here. Careful now. That's it.' She held the pup back by its tail as it scampered after its mother. 'Oh no you don't . . .' the woman scolded. 'she'll get no peace with you there. You'll have plenty of cuddles later. Here — there's still a drop more milk left in the bottle.'

The man glanced at his watch. 'I've got to get back

to work, love. We can decide what's to be done with them later.'

She caught his sleeve. 'How d'you mean, Ken?'

'We could talk to George Harris about it. He's calling round here for me tonight. There's a darts match down the road.'

'George? Why George?'

'Well, he's a policeman isn't he? He must have handled plenty of strays.'

His wife's jaw sagged. 'But couldn't we — er — couldn't we. . .' He pressed a finger to her lips, guessing what she was about to say. 'No, Alice,' he said firmly. 'The answer's no, we can't. So don't ask.'

'But. . .'

'Look, I'll see you at tea-time. We'll talk about it then.' He hurried out before she could say any more.

5

'Well Alice — how's the patient?'

Ken Taylor's wife hooked her arm in his and tiptoed to the hearth. The bitch — its torso swathed in bandages like a half-finished Egyptian mummy — was fast asleep. The pup dozed beside her with its head tucked underneath her hind leg. The man crouched and stroked the bitch's ear. She slowly opened one eye. 'Feeling better, old girl?' he smiled. 'I've brought you something that might help.' He strode to the kitchen and returned with a large parcel.

'Whatever's that?' asked his wife. He grinned and tore away the brown paper. 'There!' he beamed. 'Six tins of meat, a pound of mince, one packet of meal and a box of dog biscuits.' She hugged him. 'You're a love.'

They moved to the sofa. 'D'you think she's going to be OK?' he asked anxiously. His wife shrugged. 'I don't know, Ken. She hasn't stirred from there since you left. The pup's been with her all afternoon. I hadn't the heart to send it away. Anyway I think the mother wants it to be near her. She's been trying to lick its face, but the effort was too much. Mind you, both of them could certainly *do* with a wash.'

The man nodded. 'Probably still suffering from shock. I doubt if many dogs would have survived what they've been through together.' He glanced at the kitchen and began peeling off his overalls. His wife took the hint. 'Your meal's in the oven, Ken. It'll be ready when you are.'

She watched him eat for a while then nudged his arm. 'Er, by the way, have you thought about what we're going to do with them?' He grunted and carried on eating. 'Ken,' she persisted, 'you said we'd talk about it. George Harris will be round soon.'

He shook his head. 'I don't know, love. I suppose the first thing we ought to do is try to find the owners.'

'How?'

'Well, I made a few inquiries around the site this afternoon. Some of the people in neighbouring streets told me the bitch lived at the house where we found her.'

His wife clutched her cheeks. 'Good heavens, Ken. You don't mean they deliberately abandoned her. I can't believe it. No one could be so heartless.'

'Seems like it. It's happened before.'

'But where've they gone?'

'To a new council flat, I'm told. Somewhere on the other side of town. They don't allow dogs in council flats, Alice.'

'B-but surely they could have found her another home before they left. It's scandalous. They should be locked up.'

He patted her hand. 'Look, we don't know the full story. Let me have a talk with the housing department tomorrow. They're bound to know their new address. Then I'll call and see them.'

'Do we have to, Ken?'

'What d'you mean?'

'Well, couldn't we just keep them?'

He sighed impatiently. 'Now Alice . . . don't start

that again. Two dogs in a house this size just isn't on. And anyway there may be a perfectly reasonable explanation for everything.' There was a sharp rapping on the front door. 'Ah — that'll be George. I'll go.'

He returned, overshadowed by a giant of a man who crunched over the carpet with boots like bulldozers. He had to duck to enter the room. 'Evening, Alice,' he greeted. The sofa groaned as he eased himself into it. 'Starting a family, are you?' She poured him a cup of tea. 'Ken brought them home. They were left in an empty house.'

'Mm — I see. The same old story.'

'How do you mean, George?'

'It's happening all the time. Someone moves into a new place. Or the wife's having a baby. Or they're going on holiday. Suddenly the dog's in the way. They haven't the guts to bring them to us. It's easier just to ditch them.'

The woman closed her eyes. 'Oh George, that's awful. That really is. Can't you do something about it?'

'We just haven't the time, love. D'you realise how many strays there are in this country? Nearly a quarter of a million. Take Christmas for instance. The kids pester their parents for a pet. Everyone makes a big fuss of it. Then it starts growing up. It chews things. It needs more food. It has to be taken for walks. Then there's the licence. Suddenly it's a problem and it's got to go.'

The policeman grew angrier as he went on. 'You'd be sickened if you'd seen what happens to some of these wretched creatures. I've known them to be flung from moving cars or tethered to the side of some lonely country road. We found one dog with its front legs lashed together so it couldn't chase after its owner's car.

'Some of them are so faithful, too. A year ago we picked up a dog on the grass verge of a busy trunk road. A lorry driver actually saw a man throw it a stick, then jump into his car and drive away as the animal ran to retrieve it. Do you know, that dog curled up beside the stick and wouldn't budge. Three days it was there, until the same lorry driver reported it on his return journey. It still believed its owner would come back. It was starving when we took it in. I tell you, I'm not soft about animals, but that sort of thing makes my blood boil.'

The woman listened open-mouthed, shaking her head and occasionally calling over her shoulder: 'Did you hear that, Ken?'

The policeman levered himself from the sofa. 'Sorry if I've upset you, Alice. But I do get a bit mad when the subject crops up.'

He put his huge arm over her shoulders. 'Anyway, the thing is, what are you going to do with those two? D'you want me to take them to the dogs' home?'

She glanced at the bitch. 'What happens there, George?'

'They keep them for a week to see if anyone claims them.'

'Then what?'

'Well — you know — they're put down.'

'Put down,' she repeated softly, still watching the bitch. 'Put to sleep?'

'There's no other way. What else could they do with them? New ones are brought in every day. They don't feel anything.'

'How do you *know* they don't? How can you be sure? How can anyone be sure?'

George shuffled his enormous feet. 'Well, I don't think they do.'

For most of this time the woman's husband had said nothing. But when she glanced at his pained expression it was obvious he was weakening. Suddenly he thumped his fist against the table. 'Right,' he scowled, 'that settles it. I've heard enough. We'll keep the little perishers.' He flung on his jacket. 'Now come on George, we'll be late for darts.'

As the men left, the woman noticed her husband brush his eye with his sleeve. She gave the bitch a smug wink. 'Well love,' she whispered, 'it worked.'

After seven days of good food and devoted attention from Ken and Alice Taylor, the bitch fully recovered and the pup was beginning to accept that perhaps the world wasn't such a bad place after all.

The man had bought a cosy wicker basket big enough for them to snuggle in together by the hearth. He had also put a brand new collar round the older dog's neck and was already taking her for short walks on a shiny leather lead. The animals were barely recognisable from the filthy, unkempt creatures he had brought home a week ago. The bitch — bathed and brushed until her coat shone — was bright-eyed and alert, grooming and fussing her pup, cuffing it occasionally when it got out of hand as it followed her everywhere.

The woman had borrowed a book on dogs from the public library. She was engrossed in it now, staring hard at the bitch from time to time, then referring to illustrations in the book. 'Well,' asked her husband, 'what d'you think?'

'She seems to be a bit of everything,' she sighed. 'There's some collie in her, that's for sure. Look at her head.' She prodded the book with her podgy finger. 'See Ken. Small eyes and sharpish nose. Yes, there's definitely some collie there. Then there's her tail. Collies have long tails like that. Yes, I'm sure that's what she is. They're very intelligent, you know.'

He shook his head. 'In that case it must be the smallest collie in the world. Why, it's no bigger than a fox terrier.'

'Perhaps she's a miniature collie. You know, like they have miniature poodles.'

'Don't be daft Alice.'

He tried to read a newspaper.

'Ken.'

'Yes Alice?'

'What about this one?'

'Which?'

She pushed the book under his nose. 'This . . .'

He reeled back. 'A Portuguese Warren Hound! What the devil's that?'

'Well, there are similarities. It says here they have long tails and triangular ears and come in three different sizes.'

He shoved the book away and retreated behind his newspaper. For a while his wife muttered to herself. 'Mm, mind you there's a touch of golden retriever about the body. Well, in patches anyway. Of course if the legs were thicker they could be cocker spaniel's . . .' She brushed aside her husband's paper. 'What do *you* think, Ken?'

He sighed wearily. 'Look love, let's face it. It's nothing special — just an ordinary everyday run-of-the-mill mongrel.'

His wife flung her arms round the bitch's neck. 'Well, I don't care. I think she's lovely. Anyway mongrels are more faithful than all those fancy breeds. Everyone knows that. I'm glad she is a mongrel.'

'Ken,' she murmured a few minutes later, emerging from her book.

'Yes?'

'D'you think it's a Polish Sheepdog?'

He leapt from his chair at the sound of the front door knocker. 'Thank heavens,' he growled, 'it's George.'

The moment the policeman stomped into the room the bitch's back arched and prickled like a porcupine's. Her lips curled over her teeth and twitched as she growled and drew away. The woman rushed to pacify her. 'There, there love. What's all this about then? It's only George. He won't harm you.'

'That's funny,' puzzled the policeman. 'I usually get on well with dogs.'

'Perhaps it's those big feet of yours,' teased the woman.

Actually it was his feet. Or rather the boots. For a moment the bitch was reminded of that terrible day she cowered in the cubby-hole listening to boots just like those grinding up the stairs. But she mellowed when he dipped into his overcoat pocket and produced the biggest bone she'd ever seen. In fact the pup had to vacate its place in the basket to make room for it as its mother heaved it over the rim. 'She's only small,' chuckled the policeman, 'but she's not short of guts, I'll say that for her.'

The woman glowed with pride. 'Yes,' said her

husband profoundly, 'it's in the breed, George.'

'Oh?'

'Yes — it's a Portuguese Warren Hound you know.'

'A what?'

'With a touch of Polish Sheepdog.'

'You're kidding!'

'Well that's what the wife says.'

The men roared as she pushed them through the front door. 'That's enough of that Ken. Go on — out, both of you. You'll miss your precious darts.'

The moment they'd gone she grabbed the library book again, picked up the pup and placed it next to her on the sofa. 'Right,' she said eagerly, 'now let's get you sorted out.'

6

For the next few weeks the pup really got its milk teeth into the rugged business of growing up. On an energy-packed diet of milk and raw eggs it became stronger, livelier and more self-confident every day, tearing about the Taylors' small terraced home on gangling legs until it would skid out of control across the polished floor like a curling stone on ice, crunching soft and seemingly unbreakable bones against the walls. The woman would catch her breath and cover her face. But the crazy little animal would merely sneeze and totter back to the basket to re-focus its eyes. It constantly craved affection from the couple as it sprawled between them on the sofa.

Despite her new-found comfort and security the bitch, however, was strangely restless. At night she hardly slept and, during the day, would lie for hours, muzzle flat on the floor, and ears pricked as if searching for sounds that were far removed from the confines of the little living-room. Whenever the man took her out she would constantly sniff the ground and tug the lead. Something — some nagging instinct — was badgering her to return to the derelict house.

In terms of human logic this, of course, made no sense at all. Here, with the warm-hearted Taylors, there was everything she and her pup would ever need. Why then should she want to go back there... to emptiness and hunger and a dark dungeon under the stairs?

But logic played no part in what she felt. Only cold, primitive instinct. The instinct of a dog that still believed its original owners would return. Like that dog the policeman had told the Taylors about. The one that waited for days at the roadside guarding a stick. The bitch, too, felt committed to wait at the old house however long the vigil. Time didn't matter. It was her duty to be there when they did come back.

Of course human beings could never have understood. 'I think she's sickening for something,' the woman said. She had taken her to the vet who'd given her pills, but they made no difference. 'Still suffering from shock,' was all her husband could suggest. And, as it seemed the only likely conclusion, they had settled for that.

The pup was almost three months old when the bitch saw her chance... It was the morning the refuse men called. The woman was chatting to a neighbour across the street. The scullery door was off its latch when the dog heard the backyard gate squeak open and saw one of the men heave the heavy metal waste bin onto his ox-like shoulders. He returned, clattering the empty bin in its usual place. As he left, the gate swung back against the black-painted spring. But, instead of clicking shut, it stopped against the dustbin handle, leaving a gap of about a foot.

The bitch nosed open the unlatched scullery door and walked out across the flagstones, slipping easily through the gap and into the cobbled passage beyond.

The pup followed as far as the yard gate then halted and looked round. The blustery February wind gathered up scattered cinder dust from the bin and flung it into its screwed-up face. As it started back towards the house its mother thrust her head round the gate and barked impatiently. The pup glanced over its shoulder then sat down facing the older dog. For a few moments they stared at each other. The pup could hear the woman's faint voice across the street and wanted to scamper back into the scullery with its warm, soupy smell. As if leaving it to make its own momentous decision, the bitch turned her back on the bewildered pup and walked away. The youngster still hesitated, but only for a moment. Then it gave a sharp cry and shot into the passage after its mother, coming alongside of her as she turned the corner into the street.

Side by side they trotted briskly on, the bitch bustling her offspring close to the house walls, nudging it firmly with her body if it began to wander. Occasionally she stopped dead, prodding her nose into the wind before darting off in some other direction. When a street had to be crossed the traffic-conscious bitch held back her impetuous pup by the scruff of its neck until she knew it was safe.

After an hour or so the streets broadened. There were fewer houses, and these were tucked away behind towering hedges. There were trees instead of lamp-posts — fingering the sky that now seemed much nearer than before. It was colder too, and when stray snowflakes pirouetted by, the pup snapped the air to catch them.

By midday there were no buildings, only open fields stretching on forever beyond the winding roadside hedges. It was snowing hard now and the wind raked the dogs' fur until the pup could barely keep its feet. It was frightened and confused. Where were they going . . . and why?

Long before this they had, of course, become

hopelessly lost. But there was little point in turning back. They had made so many detours their departure point could have been in any direction. So the determined bitch struggled blindly on, still believing that some familiar scent would manifest itself and guide them to where she knew she had to go.

An hour later the road narrowed to a few yards, seeming to burrow its way between hedgerows now billowing white with a fresh blossom of puffy snow. Soon there was no road at all — just a deep crisp carpet being munched beneath their paws. But the wind had died and the sun burst through, garnishing the frosty branches with shimmering tinsel . . . making every tree a Christmas tree. To the pup it suddenly became a new and exciting world that had to be explored.

Ignoring the bitch's scolding growls, the pup bounded off frog-like through the snow — rolling in it, licking it, shovelling it with its nose and swiping it with its paws. The inquisitive youngster crouched beside a hedge to watch a sparrow with a white feather sprouting from its beak like a handlebar moustache. As it watched, the crooked arm of a great oak creaked overhead and a powdery avalanche thundered down. The pup yelped and leapt to its guardian's side, panting winter mist and showering her with its own little snowstorm. The bitch licked its wet face as they rested for a while. But she still savoured the tingling air in her twitching nostrils for those elusive clues so very far away.

As the afternoon sun melted into the branches of the trees, long black talons of shadow clawed the shrouded fields. The older dog shook herself and pushed on, turning back every now and then at the pup galumphing along behind. But the bitch was tiring rapidly and slackened her pace to a slow limp. Her muscles ached and she could hardly lift her heavy limbs through the grasping snow. Weary and confused, she had to rest again.

Meanwhile the pup snuffled on along a hedgerow. Even a hungry stomach couldn't dull its even hungrier curiosity. It had to find out more about this extraordinary world. What, for instance, lay on the other side of the hedgerow?

With a thrust, a wriggle and a squirm it found out. There was a large field, in it were creatures much like herself. They had four legs and a tail like herself, except that they were white and woolly like the snow and, instead of barking, they made soft throbbing sounds that seemed full of sadness.

The pup crept nearer, panting excitedly with ears jutting forward. A few moments later it was in amongst them, sniffing their black feet then leaping backwards urging them to romp. When they scattered with jerky, frolicsome bounds, the pup did the same, yapping gaily at their heels.

The bitch peered under the hedge sensing danger and the pup didn't notice her suddenly burst through it and start across the field. But it heard the shuddering crack and spun round to see her being tossed backwards into the air as if an invisible tripwire had lashed across her throat. She crashed onto her side, twitched once or twice, and lay still as birds swept screaming from the trees like confetti. The pup was transfixed. An instant later something thumped into its own hind leg sending it sprawling to the ground as another sharp blast echoed across the field. A stab of burning pain raked the pup's body. It trembled and gasped for breath.

Now a man was climbing the hedge, cradling something in his arms. It glinted in the orange sun and a faint shadow of smoke curled away from one end. The man strode over to the bitch and turned her limp body with the toe of his knee-high leather boot. A patch of blood streaked the snow. He put a hand to her chest and grunted.

The pup stared wildly about and saw that another hedge crossed the field only a yard or two away. It watched the man break the long shiny object across his knee and fumble for something in his jacket pocket. Struggling to its feet, it lurched towards the hedge trailing one helpless leg through the snow. It collapsed, gulped air, and tried again. The man was still some distance away. As he moved nearer, the pup dragged itself on and scrabbled into the hedge, crying in anguish as the clutching branches tried to claw it back, ripping away tufts of soft fur by the roots. Finally, with a mad flurry of terror, it was through. As it lay trembling on the other side the ground beneath it suddenly gave way and the startled animal toppled over and over down a steep bank showering itself with snow until a small bush broke the fall.

The injured leg throbbed as the pup furrowed aside the fur with its tongue and gingerly explored the torn raw flesh. It could hear the man cursing as he thrust apart the hedge with his hands and prodded with his boot. But it was thick and tightly woven. He knew he could not get through and it was too high to climb. Another man ran across the field to join him. 'The dog over there's dead all right,' he shouted. 'Did you get this one?'

'Don't know. Thought I had. The varmint's behind here somewhere. Come on, we can get round by the next field.'

The pup whined softly, flinching with pain as it made a feeble effort to haul itself up the bank, but it was useless. There was no way it could impel its cramped muscles to respond. Very slowly it slid backwards down the slope, its chin ploughing the snow, until a shallow stream lapped its hind legs drawing away a red stain. The icy water probed the open wound with agonising suddenness that stiffened the pup's flagging body. As its front paws stabbed the snow a chunk of it fell away revealing the mouth of a small round tunnel in the bank. Barely conscious, it strained forward, claws groping ahead for cracks in the bone-hard ground. Once inside, it inched along by arching its back caterpillar-fashion. The tunnel narrowed and hugged the animal close. Then it turned off at right-angles. The pup twisted round it with a final tortuous heave and lay still listening to the dull throb of men's voices.

'This is about where the little devil came through. Yes, look — blood stains. I *did* clip him.'

Heavy boots churned the crisp snow at the tunnel entrance.

'Hey, hold on!'

'What?'

'This warren. D'you think it's in here?'

'It's a bit narrow. Just a minute . . .'

The pup jerked back and froze as the muzzle of a shotgun thudded against solid earth a few inches from its nose.

'Nothing here.'

'It's losing blood. We should be able to trace it.'

'Yes, there's a smear down here.'

'Where?'

'Here — near the stream.'

'Curses, it must have crossed into the field on the other side. Come on.'

The pup heard thrashing water and then the voices again, a little fainter this time.

'That's odd . . . no paw marks over here.'

'Then it must have run through the stream and climbed the bank further down.'

There was silence for a moment. 'Blast it, it could be anywhere by now.'

'Never mind. Reckon it won't worry any more sheep in a hurry. Come on, let's go. It'll be dark in another couple of hours. We've plenty to do back at the farm.'

'Maybe you're right.'

As the grumbling voices faded, the pup crawled a few feet along the tunnel and lay staring out, sniffing the cold air.

7

Instinct urged the pup to leave the tunnel. The men might return. It needed food, too. Then it remembered the gunfire and its mother lying motionless in the snow somewhere on the other side of the hedge. It was her it needed most of all. She'd know what to do as she always did. Perhaps she was still there.

The pup tried to creep through the tunnel opening but even its undamaged legs doubled up at the first movement and it rolled back helplessly, lolling its tongue between drooling lips and gasping with long raking breaths.

Then the desperate little animal howled. With all the power left in its tortured lungs, it howled — almost as if surrendering to the men with the gun. But it was the only way it knew of calling to the bitch out there. The fact that others might hear the baleful sound was beyond its simple reasoning. But others did . . .

Suddenly the snow rustled outside. The pup stopped howling and listened. A pair of small black boots appeared at the tunnel opening only a couple of feet from its nose.

'It's coming from in here, Elsie.' The voice was nothing like those of the men — more of a chirrup that rippled like the stream below. The second voice was much the same and came in a whisper . . .

'Shush Jenny, you'll scare it.'

'Scare what?'

'Whatever's in there, of course.'

'Look inside Elsie.'

'Ooh no, I'm scared.'

'Don't be daft. Move over — I'll look.'

A moment later the pup found itself staring into a dimply face with wide blue eyes and a glowing nose — all held together by a thick wooly muffler tied in a knot at the top. It gave a squeal and vanished. 'Oh Elsie . . . Elsie . . .'

'What Jenny, what?'

'There *is* something in there.'

'Oo-er.'

'Oh come back, you idiot.'

'What is it?'

'It's small and furry.'

'Oh is that all. It's only a rabbit. Fancy being scared of a rabbit.'

'I don't think so. Just a minute.' The pup whimpered as the face reappeared. 'It's a dog, Elsie.'

'It can't be. Dogs don't live in holes.'

'Well this one does.'

'Has it got big ears?'

'Sort of.'

'Then it's a rabbit.' A second face peered into the tunnel. It was pale and freckled like breadcrumbs in the snow. 'Oh Jenny, you're right. It is a dog.'

'Told you, didn't I.' The cherry lips puckered and the child clucked her tongue. 'Come on then . . .' she purred coaxingly. 'Come on — we won't hurt you.'

Small, chubby fingers crept along the tunnel and the pup cringed and sneezed when they touched its nose. It sniffed them cautiously. They stretched further and caressed its head. Smooth, gentle fingers they were. And when they carefully took hold of the fur at the back of its neck and drew it forward, the weary little dog made no effort to resist. It hadn't the strength. Besides, anything was better than staying there alone under the cold earth.

The girl's lap was warm and soft and the pup's ear flipped as she brushed it with her cheek. 'Look Jenny, it's only a baby.'

As her sister stroked along its side, the pup's head jerked in a spasm of pain. 'Oh Jenny, Jenny — it's hurt. The poor creature's hurt. It's been bleeding. See — there, all down its back leg.'

'Perhaps it's been attacked.'

'But who'd attack a helpless thing like this?'

'Something wild and ferocious.'

'Like a fox?'

'No, wilder than that.'

'What then?'

'An eagle.'

'An eagle?'

'Yes. Sometimes eagles attack pups and carry them off in their claws. Aw — look. It's asleep. It must be worn out.'

'What're we going to do with it, Jenny?'

'Well, we can't take it home, that's for sure. You know how Mam and Dad are about having animals in the house. 'Specially dogs.'

'Yes, I know. They make Mam ill. What was it Dad said she had?'

'An allergy.'

'That's right — an allergy.'

'So what are we going to do? It's getting dark. We can't leave it here. What if the eagle comes back?'

They watched the pup for a while saying nothing except 'aah' and tilting their heads from side to side.

'I know what we'll do.'
'What Jenny?'
'Take it to the barn.'
'But what if Dad finds out?'
'He won't if we're careful. He hasn't been in there for weeks. It's warm and there's plenty of straw.'
'You *sure* it'll be all right?'
''Course I am. Now come on, it's meal-time. Dad'll be out looking for us and then that'll be that.'
It took ten minutes to reach the barn and the pup's injured leg throbbed painfully each step of the way as it curled in Jenny's arms. Elsie ran on ahead to check there was no one in the rickety old wooden building as her sister crouched by the barred gate shielding the pup with her coat. At a signal from the other girl she hurried across the farmyard and slipped through the barn door.
The pup's nostrils quivered at new and magical smells — like the heady tang of creosote and cow-dung, of dry straw and rotting timber. The children laid it gently in a corner after first ruffling together a deep bed of clean straw. 'There,' said Jenny maternally. 'That's better, isn't it?' She turned to whisper to Elsie as though the pup might interpret what she was saying. 'We must see to that wound.'
'How?'
'It's got to be cleaned. I know where Mam keeps the lint and things. And we'll need some hot water and that stuff in the blue bottle Mam puts on cuts.'
'But it's meal-time Jenny. They won't let us out again.'
'Yes they will. We'll come back *after* tea. We always do anyway to feed the rabbit.'
'Oh yes, that's right.'
They both patted the pup's head. 'There,'

whispered Jenny. 'Now pet, we won't be long. We'll bring you some food and we'll try to make you better.' Then they both crept out.

'And about time too, young ladies.'

The man eating at the kitchen table was big and rugged, his face leathered by the changing seasons of a lifetime on the bleak moorland around the rambling stone farmhouse. The woman beside him was as round and wholesome as a cottage loaf. 'Where've you been till now?' she snapped. 'You know very well I want you home before dark.' Jenny washed her hands at the big brown sink. 'Sorry Mam.'

'Never mind sorry Mam. You'll have to talk to them John,' grumbled their mother, rattling two more plates onto the rough wooden table. 'It's not good enough. They just don't listen to me.' The man yawned. He knew she'd say that. He'd talk to them some other time when he felt less tired. 'Later Maggie, later,' he said irritably.

As the girls slid sheepishly to their places together at the table, the woman knelt before an enormous black oven twiddling the brass knob like a frustrated safe-breaker. 'Damn the monstrosity!' she cried. 'When are you going to fix this pesky door, John? It's been like this for weeks.' He opened his mouth to speak. 'I know, I know,' she went on, '. . . tomorrow. It's always tomorrow.'

Jenny nudged her sister. 'She's in a bad mood, Elsie,' she hissed behind her hand. 'Hope she'll let us out afterwards.'

Their mother finally found the right combination for the faulty knob and creaked open the oven door, heaving out a huge earthenware dish from which she ladled piping hot stew onto the girls' plates. 'And make sure you eat every scrap,' chided the woman, 'you need full stomachs this weather.' The sisters winked at each other. There'd be plenty left for the dog. The woman scraped the rest of the stew onto her husband's plate. 'After rabbits this afternoon, were you?' she asked him casually. 'I heard the shotgun.'

'No Maggie — dogs.'

'Dogs?'

Jenny gave a strangled cry.

'What's the matter with you?' growled her father.

'N-nothing Dad,' stuttered Jenny, grasping Elsie's skinny knee under the table and making her drop her fork with a clatter.

'What dogs?' asked their mother.

'Killers, that's what.'

'What happened?'

He continued eating for a moment as the girls held their breath. 'Bob and I saw them chasing the sheep. We killed one all right. The other ran off, but I winged it. Don't think it'll get far.'

Jenny choked on a mouthful of stew. 'For heaven's sake, child — what is the matter with you?' demanded her father. Her bottom lip quivered. 'But why? How could you Dad? How could you? A little thing like . . .' Elsie's sharp nails dug into her leg and she checked herself.

He sighed impatiently. 'I'll tell you why, Jenny. Because I've seen sheep after a dog's finished with them. It's not a pretty sight. If folk can't keep their pets under control they deserve to lose them. I'm not blaming the dogs. After all they're descended from wolves, I suppose. They may be harmless enough curled up on a rug by the fire, but once they're left to run wild the instinct to hunt and kill is still there.'

Jenny pursed her lips, trying not to cry. 'But Dad,

how do you know the dogs you shot were like that? What if they weren't? What if they were just playful?'

'I wasn't taking that chance, my girl. And I'll tell you another thing. If the one that got away ever comes back . . .' He drove his clenched fist against the table top making the pots jump, and the girls too. 'I'll make sure next time.'

Jenny gripped her knife and fork until her small hands shook. 'I hate you . . . I *hate* you,' she blurted, bursting into tears.

Her father stared back in disbelief as his wife threw up her hands. '*Jenny* — how dare you talk to your father like that? How *dare* you?'

'B-but it's wicked and horrible, Mam.'

'Would you sooner we lost half the sheep, you stupid girl?'

The man patted his wife's arm. 'All right Maggie, don't get yourself all worked up. She doesn't understand. Kids never do.' He nudged his plate away. 'Now let's forget it. There's nothing more to be said.' He withdrew a heavy gold pocket-watch from his waistcoat and grimaced. 'Ugh — is that the time? I'm off, Maggie. See you later.'

'Never mind the pub. What about my oven door?'

'Don't worry, don't worry — it'll be done.' He ruffled Jenny's mousy hair. 'And don't you worry that young head of yours about things that don't concern you. You'll understand when you're a bit older.' As she instinctively drew away, he dragged on his overcoat and left.

His wife snapped her fingers. 'Now then you two, get that food down before it goes cold. I'm going to tidy up the front room. I don't want to see a thing on those plates when I come back.' She flicked Jenny's shoulder with the back of her hand. 'And stop blubbering child — your father knows best about these things.'

As she flounced out of the room Elsie threw her arms round her sister. 'Oh Jenny,' she cried, 'd'you think Dad means what he said? D'you think he'd really kill the pup?' The other girl stared past her. 'Yes, I do.'

'What're we going to do? What if he finds out?'

Jenny sniffed and set her jaw. 'We've just got to make sure he doesn't.'

'But we can't keep it in the barn forever. He's bound to go in there sometime.'

'Oh Elsie — I don't know. Don't keep on so! We'll think of something. Meanwhile we've got to feed the poor thing and attend to that leg.'

She hurried into the scullery for a dish into which she emptied the leftover stew from their plates. Then she tip-toed upstairs to the bathroom, returning with lint and a bottle of antiseptic lotion. She filled another dish with warm water from a kettle on the stove. All of these items she laid carefully on the step outside the back door, then sat down at the table as her mother bustled in, sweeping away the sisters' plates. Jenny waited a few minutes then tugged Elsie's skirt. As they walked towards the back door their mother glowered at them over her shoulder. 'And where d'you think you're off to now?' Jenny grabbed a paper bag from the shelf on the wall. 'To feed the rabbit, Mam.'

'It's too late.'

The sister's gaped at each other.

'But Mam,' pleaded Elsie. 'We haven't fed it for hours.' Her mother ignored her and slid the plates into the bubbly washing-up water. 'Please Mam,' pestered Jenny.

Red hands clattered the swirling pots around the sink. 'Please Mam, please.'

The woman slapped a dishcloth into the water as the girls ducked from the soapy spray. 'Oh for goodness sake . . .' Jenny dragged her sister outside. 'Thanks Mam, we won't be long — honest.'

The pup was asleep when they crept into the barn. Jenny knelt beside it and stroked away the short silky fur on either side of the torn flesh. The pup twitched but its eyes remained closed. 'We'll try not to hurt you,' consoled Jenny. 'But you've got to be brave. It's for your own good.' She soaked some lint in the warm water and bathed away the dark, dry blood. The pup protested softly and tried to pull away.

The wound was only superficial but it looked like raw meat and Elsie rolled her blue eyes. 'Oh Jenny,' she moaned, 'I think I'm going to faint.' Her sister dug her in the ribs. 'You'd better not,' she threatened.

'But it makes me go all funny.'

'Well shut your eyes then.'

She did. 'D'you think it'll live?'

'Idiot. 'Course it'll live. It's not serious. It looks much worse than it really is.' She dripped lotion onto a fresh piece of lint and carefully dabbed the wound. 'There, it's all over now. It'll lick it better when it feels stronger.' She reached for the dish of stew and placed it by the pup's head, but it made no attempt to eat. 'We'll leave it here Elsie,' she said. 'Now we've got to get back to the house before Mam comes looking for us.'

Both girls bent down and kissed the pup's ear. Then they hitched up their woollen stockings and dusted straw from their skirts. 'See you tomorrow,' called back Jenny as they left.

8

The sunlight of a tingling new winter day spread across the tousled carpet of straw, melting the sleep from the pup's sticky eyes. Mother Nature had nursed the little animal diligently during the long night, tidying up the wound and soothing shattered nerves as only she can. To build up her patient's resistance she was now nagging it to fill its empty stomach. The dish of stew smelt delicious. But when the pup stretched its legs there was a sharp reminder not to rush things as the wound snagged and made it cry out. So, instead of trying to stand, it curled a paw over the edge of the dish and lapped the spilt gravy out of the straw. It stopped abruptly as the barn door groaned.

'Morning!' piped Jenny. 'Oh look Elsie, it's eating the stew.' The pup tried to wag its tail but it hurt, so it just panted excitedly. The girls hurried to the dog's side. Jenny pushed a saucer of warm milk under its nose and her sister unwrapped an egg from a napkin. When the pup had finished the milk she cracked the shell and emptied the gooey contents into the saucer. Jenny beamed. 'It must be getting better. Look how hungry it is. That's a sure sign.'

'Shall I give it another egg?'

'Why not.'

The pup gobbled up that one, too. Elsie watched,

frowning and cocking her head. 'Jenny,' she said at last.

'Yes?'

'What d'you think it is?'

'What d'you mean, what do I think it is? It's a puppy of course.'

'No, what sort?'

'Oh a mongrel I should think.'

'No, I mean is it a boy or a girl?'

'It's a girl,' declared Jenny emphatically.

'How d'you know?'

'Well, er — it looks like one.'

'Why?'

'Oh, does it matter, Elsie?'

'Well I think it's a boy. You can tell by it's face.'

'Rubbish!'

'I still say it's a boy.'

'Look Elsie, I should know. I'm ten. I'm a year older than you.'

'Oh, you're very clever, you are. But go on — tell me how you know.'

Jenny considered the challenge for a moment then gently turned the pup over, being very careful not to jar the injured leg. 'There!' she cried triumphantly, 'what did I tell you . . . no John Willie. That means it's a girl.' Which seemed conclusive enough even for Elsie, who modestly lowered her eyes. 'That's rude,' was all she could think of to say. Jenny gave a scornful toss of her head. 'Oh honestly you're such a child sometimes, you really are.' She returned her attention to the pup. 'Now little girl, what are we going to do with you?' she asked it. Elsie tapped her arm. 'What time will Mam and Dad be back from the village, Jenny?'

'Oh not for hours. They've left us a cold lunch and

Auntie Doris is coming round this afternoon. She always does on Saturdays, so they'll be glad to have us out of the way. It's Monday that bothers me. What'll happen to it when we're at school?'

'Perhaps we can find it somewhere else to hide — somewhere well away from the farm.'

Jenny didn't appear to be listening as a tear trickled down her cheek. 'What's the matter?' her sister asked.

'Nothing Elsie. I was just thinking.'

'About what?'

'About that other dog. The one Dad shot. Supposing it was this one's mother.'

'Oh no.'

'It could have been.'

'Oh Jenny, that's terrible. It must be wondering where she is.'

Jenny thought for a moment. 'It might have a collar with a name and address on it. Older dogs usually do. Then we could take the pup to its owner.'

'But how can we find out?'

'Go and look at it, you nitwit. How else?'

'Ugh — but it's dead. Dad said so.'

'Oh you really are the end, Elsie.'

'But how d'you know where the dog is — or even if it's still there?'

'I don't. So we've got to go and find out, haven't we?'

'If you say so,' muttered Elsie swallowing hard.

The children found the bitch. She was still lying in the field, stiff and dusted with powdered snow. There was a collar round its thin neck, but no name or address. So they left it there and sobbed all the way back to the farm.

By Sunday morning the pup was much stronger and could hobble about the barn poking its nose into the corners. It could thump its tail against the floor whenever the children crept in with food — all mufflers and mittens and winter baubles dripping from their noses. Pain still niggled the injured hind leg, but not enough to stop the pup wanting to play whenever the girls ruffled the straw.

'It's school tomorrow,' reminded Elsie. Her sister sighed. 'Yes, I know. I've been trying to think of something all day.'

'If we just had a place to hide it while we were away we could still let it sleep here.'

'Yes, Elsie — but where?'

'What about that hollow at the bottom of the big tree down the lane? The one where we keep our conkers.'

'Oh sure. And I suppose it's going to just sit there patiently all day waiting for us . . . I don't think.'

'All right smarty-pants — you think of a better place then,' sulked Elsie.

'It's got to be inside somewhere where it can't get out. I know . . . we'll take it to school.'

'What!'

'Look, there's a shed where they keep the sports equipment. No one'll be using it this weather. I know where the key is. It's on a hook in the corridor.'

'Bit risky, isn't it?'

'Not if we get there early, before the teachers.' Jenny looked guiltily at the pup. 'You'll be all right, love, really you will. It's only till we find somewhere better.'

The woman pushed a plate of sizzling bacon and eggs across the kitchen table as her husband tapped the face of his pocket-watch. 'Damn,' he muttered, 'it's stopped again. What's the time Maggie?' She checked the grandfather clock ticking ponderously in the living-room. 'It's eight o'clock.'

'Damn,' he said again. 'I've got to go into town this morning.' His wife poured tea into a thick pint pot at his elbow. He sipped it tentatively between his teeth, making drain-like noises as he struck the offending watch against the table edge.

'That'll do it a power of good,' said his wife dryly. 'Anyway, what're you going to town for?'

'To get rid of that blooming transformer. It's faulty. I phoned yesterday. The firm say they'll exchange it if I take it in.' He mopped the bacon fat with a crust. 'The kids are late. Aren't they going to school this morning?'

'They've been up for ages, John. They're out feeding the rabbit.'

'That's odd. We've usually got to drag them out of bed.'

'That's what I thought.'

The man dismissed the matter with a shrug. 'I'll just go and load up. I'll take the car. The transformer should fit in the boot.'

'Where is it?'

'In the barn.'

The sisters were thrilled with the pup's progress. Apart from the limp, it appeared to have made a complete recovery. Elsie cracked open a raw egg and chuckled as the lively little dog guzzled it down almost before it hit the saucer. 'She's fine now Jenny.'

'Yes, I don't think she'll come to any harm in the sports shed for a few hours. We can leave her some food and nip across between lessons. Better come and get ready now. We can pick her up on the way out.'

'Jenny!'

'What is it?'

'Listen...'

The girls held their breath, wide eyes trained on the barn door. The slow unmistakable crunch of heavy boots across the snow-covered yard drew nearer.

'It's Dad!'

'Oh no, Jenny. What'll we do?'

'Quick — hide it. Under the straw.'

Elsie frantically scraped out a hole as her sister dropped the pup inside, scooping the straw back over the top of it. The footsteps shuffled outside the door. Jenny snatched the saucer and rammed it under the straw too. Elsie gripped her wrist tight as the latch clicked. 'Stop shaking,' snapped Jenny, 'you'll give the game away.' Elsie gritted her teeth and wanted to be sick.

The barn door grated open and the monolithic frame of their father, haloed by the glare of sun on his back, towered over them. His eyes narrowed. 'And what are *you* pair up to?' he demanded. Jenny positioned herself between him and the buried pup. 'Nothing Dad.'

'Nothing eh? I can tell by Elsie's face you've been up to *something*.' Jenny smiled weakly and gave her sister a sharp prod on the shin with her heel. 'She's just seen a mouse, Dad. You know what she's like about mice. I've told her they're harmless.' Their father scraped his chin. 'Mm. You sure that's all it is?'

''Course Dad.'

'Anyway, hadn't you better be getting off to school?'

The heavy metal transformer he'd come for stood

against the far wall. As he turned towards it, the straw behind Jenny stirred. Elsie gaped. An instant later there was a muffled sneeze and up flew a puff of dry straw. The man swung round. 'What's that?' Jenny whipped a handkerchief from her pocket and patted her small red nose. 'Hay-fever,' she croaked with a sick smile.

'Hay-fever, girl? In the middle of winter?' The straw rippled. Elsie saw it out of the corner of her eye and her throat grew tight until it hurt. A small white paw snaked out, twitched, then drew back again. She stopped breathing.

'You ill or something, Elsie?'

'N-no Dad.'

He frowned, searching the faces of both girls. Then he strode across the floor. 'Kids!' he mumbled shaking his head. He heaved the transformer into his gorilla-like arms and humped it through the door. 'Now get off to school both of you, d'you hear?'

Elsie stared after him looking as though she would keel over any second, as her sister brushed aside the straw. The pup was cowering and trembling vigorously. 'There, that's a good girl,' calmed Jenny. 'It was a near thing though, wasn't it?' She slapped the other girl's bony knee, jerking her back to life. 'For goodness sake, Elsie, it's all right now. He's gone.'

She smoothed the pup's fur. 'Ah, what's the matter love? You're still shaking like a leaf.' It had every reason to do so. The footsteps and the man's voice had struck terror into its pounding heart. It had recognised them. They reminded it of the gun; of its mother somersaulting in the snow; and of itself lying helpless in that dark hole by the stream.

'Jenny . . . Elsie . . . do you know what time it is?' The

shrill urgency of their mother's voice hustled the sisters to the barn door. 'Coming, Mam!' yelled Jenny, glancing back at the pup and putting a finger to her lips. 'Be back in a minute, pet.'

As soon as the girls left, the pup scrambled out of the straw, shook itself and limped to the door. It had to get away before the man came back. It cautiously sniffed the icy air outside. The misshapen farm implements scattered about the yard had been sculpted into things of grace and beauty by a fresh fall of snow during the night. Clusters of sparrows, fearless with hunger, were squabbling over breadcrumbs. Otherwise the yard was clear. The dog, still trembling, waited a moment longer then scurried across and out of the farm gate. It stopped in its tracks. An old, weatherbeaten motor car was parked a few feet away and, climbing awkwardly out of it was the man, his huge leather boots creaking the long grass that had been honed crisp and knife-edged by the frost.

The dog stared in panic. There was no way it could run without being seen. Then it glanced up. The boot or the trunk of the car was open. It was strewn with potato sacks. With one wild leap that sent a ripping pain through its body, the pup was inside and burrowing underneath them. The man picked up the transformer from beside the gate and lugged it to the car, which shuddered violently as he thumped it down in the boot only an inch from the pup's nose.

'What about my oven door?' screamed a frenzied voice from the house. With a curse, the man rammed his great hands against the lid. It slammed shut with a bone-shaking crash. The pup pushed its head from under the sacking. It was pitch dark. There was an explosion and a deep-throated roar, building up to a shuddering crescendo that made the terrified pup leap forward, crunching its head against the metal shell of the car. Almost immediately it was thrown backwards as the car lurched off to a juddering grind of gears.

In the yard outside Jenny and Elsie watched the car cough and splutter out of sight, back-firing like a Roman candle. They dashed into the house and pecked their mother on the cheek. 'We're off now Mam,' cried Jenny. The woman grunted and started swiping at everything in sight with a long feather duster. 'And see you come straight home,' she ordered.

Jenny dragged her sister into the barn. They gaped at the empty hollow in the straw where they'd left the pup only a few minutes before. They clawed all round it then ran about the building squinting in corners and under farming equipment. Finally they stood blinking at each other in dismay.

'It's gone!' sobbed Jenny. 'It's gone . . .'

9

The hour-long journey in the rear of the farmer's car was a nightmare. During the first few miles over tortuous unmade roads the pup was rattled around inside like a shaken dice. It tried lying flat on its stomach, chin wedged between its feet, but was almost knocked unconscious each time the dilapidated machine struck a pot-hole. As it lurched perilously round sharp bends on its ancient springs, the rotting body appeared to be in grave danger of parting from the chassis altogether, and the pup backed away from the heavy transformer as it rocked from side to side. The noise was deafening and exhaust fumes seeped through rusty holes in the floor of the boot.

Suddenly, with a teeth-chattering judder of well-worn brakes, the car stopped. As the engine spluttered and died, a door slammed and the pup heard the dreaded footsteps. A lock clicked and a shaft of daylight stabbed the pup's eyes. It slid under the sacking as the farmer hauled out the transformer. The dog waited a second or two then peeped out to see the man hump it a few yards along the pavement and into a glass-fronted building. It filled its lungs with deep gulps of fresh air then carefully climbed backwards out of the car and limped painfully off along the street. The farmer was chatting to a white-coated assistant when he spotted the pup through the window and almost dropped the transformer. 'I don't believe it,' he gasped.

'Beg pardon, sir?'

'That dog — see it, just crossing the road now?'

'Yes sir.'

'I shot it three days ago more than twenty miles from here. Now how the blazes . . .' He heaved the transformer onto a long wooden counter. 'Damn me . . . it must have hitched a lift in my own car! I'll . . . I'll . . .'

'Sir?'

The farmer started towards the door then turned back. 'Oh what's the point. It can't get at any sheep around here, I suppose.'

'No sir, I wouldn't think it could.'

The farmer watched the assistant's perplexed expression and roared with laughter. 'The wife'll never believe it. Of all the crafty little so-and-so's.'

'No sir, I'm sure she won't,' drolled the other patiently. 'Now sir, about this transformer.'

The groggy little dog — still unable to focus its eyes properly after the buffeting ride in the car — now found itself in a world where everything seemed to be moving at ten times normal speed. Humans — dense herds of them — surged by in all directions getting in and out of each other's way and dodging wave upon wave of snarling machines that appeared intent on mowing as many of them down as they could. Everywhere the pup looked were pounding feet, bearing down on it as it wandered lop-sidedly on its gammy leg. Yet, despite the bustle, the bewildered fugitive felt lonelier than it had ever done before, and knowing its mother could certainly never find it in such a crowded place made everything seem even more frightening.

A passing foot grazed the pup's injured leg and the pain took its breath away. It turned onto a shale path and was relieved to find it led through broad stretches of short velvety grass.

There were still plenty of humans here, but instead of rushing around like confused rabbits, they were strolling leisurely or lounging on wooden benches. The pup hobbled on beyond a barrier of naked beech trees and lay beside a large ice-bound lake, idly watching a duck glide down and skid out of control across the glassy surface, bowling over a group of others like skittles. Around the fringes, the frozen lake had broken up into floating waterlilies of ice.

A woman with a basket squatted on one of the benches a few yards away. The dog watched her tear up chunks of bread and throw it about the grass. Within moments a flock of pigeons swooped in and scoffed the lot. The hungry pup edged nearer. When she dished out second helpings it leapt forward, scattering the protesting pigeons in all directions. The empty basket flew through the air, sweeping the startled pup off its feet. 'Take that, you greedy little sauce-box!' screamed the woman. 'Get away from those poor birds before I call the park-keeper. Now scat... d'you hear me!'

The pup skulked off. Humans were an unpredictable lot. You never knew how to take them. One minute they'd be saving your life and the next minute they'd be trying to blast you to Kingdom come. Only a few hours ago it had been fussed and fed on succulent raw eggs and now it was even begrudged a few measly breadcrumbs. But the dog knew that without some human charity it could not survive long. Once out of the woman's sight it lay beside a tree to shelter from the cold wind and dozed off.

It must have slept a long time. When it stretched awake the park was empty — or at least, what could be seen of it. The world seemed to have shrunk and everywhere was smoky grey. It followed the shale path into streets filled with ghosts. Soon the pup could barely see anything at all. Its eyes smarted and it had to huddle against buildings to avoid being trampled into the ground. Occasionally it tagged along hopefully behind a passer-by but could not keep up the pace. The bad leg was playing up again and was now tucked like a roast turkey's under the pup's body as it stumped along on the other three. Finally it gave up trying and staggered off along a deserted cinder-strewn road leading under a high brick archway. It curled up inside and, as its hollow stomach rumbled, the exhausted animal dreamed of happier times that seemed so very long ago.

'Good evening, little friend.'

The pup hugged the wall and bared its teeth. A hazy figure shuffled closer. 'You can stop shivering. I'm not going to hurt you.'

The dog backed away as the man held out his hand. Grubby fingers poked through frayed woollen gloves like half-peeled bananas. The pup cautiously stretched its neck and licked them. They tasted rich and meaty — good enough to eat, and it was very tempted to nip off the ends. 'There now.' It was one of those voices a dog felt it could trust. In any case, as things were, the destitute animal had to take a chance. Its tail flickered. As the man crouched on his haunches it thrust its head between his bony knees.

'That's more like it little friend. We strays must stick together, mustn't we.' The man got up and walked on a few yards. 'Over here boy.' The pup followed. Laid out beside the wall were some old blankets and a thick pile of newspapers. '*My* place,' he said waving his arm. 'Not, perhaps, what either of us may have been used to, but you're very welcome.'

He delved under the blankets and withdrew a small parcel. 'Hungry, little friend? Perhaps you'd care to join me. It isn't much, but it's filling.' The pup's eyes rolled like its stomach as the man sat against the wall and unwrapped the parcel with the aplomb of a head waiter. 'Mm — cheese again,' he said with disdain. 'That's twice this week. However . . .' He tore a thick sandwich down the middle and dropped half at the pup's feet. It pulped the offering and belched in ecstasy.

The man shared the rest of the sandwiches then dabbed his lips with the fringe of a brown jersey honeycombed with moth-holes. He dusted the cuffs of a threadbare jacket and removed his crumpled trilby hat to unfurl rippling locks of snow-white hair. The pup licked its lips and draped its throat over the man's legs. And then came a moment of sheer magic as it captured an exhilarating whiff of his feet.

A dog can learn much about Man through his feet. These were glorious. Full of character — their friendly nature pouring forth through the well-ventilated soles of his tattered shoes . . . rich and wholesome as over-ripe Stilton. It closed its eyes and sighed. It could get really attached to feet such as these. From that moment it trusted him implicitly.

The pup suddenly yelped and leapt to the man's lap. It was prompted by fright, not affection. A deafening roll of thunder threatened to bring the brick walls tumbling down about them. The man felt the soft body trembling against his chest. 'All right, all right — calm down,' he chuckled. 'You'll get used to it. You'll have to if you want to live under a railway bridge.' He felt inside a pocket of his dusty coat as the dog settled down again at his feet, and found a rucked up cigar stub which he stuffed between his lips. He scraped a match along the wall and his eyes twinkled in the flare.

'And now my little friend, allow me to introduce myself.' A deep drag at the cigar made his chin whiskers glow. 'Joseph P. Tibbles . . . actor. Tragedy, light comedy, burlesque — you name it. Late idol of the one-and-ninepennies and vaudeville's gift to the gods.' He smiled wistfully and curled the pup's ear in his fingers. 'But it's all a long time ago. Everything's changed now. The Hippodrome, the Empire, the Tivoli — they've all gone.'

He fumbled in his pocket again and withdrew a small tin box. He rapped the lid with grimy fingernails, flicked it open and pinched at something inside, snuffling it up his wide nostrils and closing his misty eyes in rapture. 'However, as you can see, I have not entirely abandoned my taste for the richer things of life.' A cold gust of wind whipped a puff of brown dust from the tin and the pup twitched its nose and sneezed as stinging tears welled from its eyes. The man grinned. 'Yes, it does take a bit of getting used to. You'll be all right in a minute.'

He slumped against the wall for a while watching the dog roll onto its side, brushing both paws across its watery eyes. Then he groped under one of the blankets. 'And now, little friend, you are about to discover the reason I live here and not at the Ritz.' He produced a bottle and screwed out the cork with his teeth. 'Whisky,' he said mournfully. 'The ruination of Joseph Tibbles.' He patted the bottle and took a long swig, wiping the dribbles from his chin with the sleeve of his coat. 'Mind you, it's medicinal too. I mean to say, on nights like this one needs more than blankets to keep warm.'

As he placed the bottle by his side the pup sniffed and licked the overspill from the glass neck. It shuddered and climbed over the man's legs. 'Ah, very prudent . . . very prudent indeed. There's an evil genie in every bottle, believe me.' He took another mouthful and gave a rusty sigh. 'Now, my little friend, I've told you my pedigree . . . what's yours? What misfortunes have made you a social misfit? Lost yourself, did you — like me?' He clicked his tongue. 'Bet you don't even have a name.'

He took another drink to consider the matter, then leaned forward and slapped his knee. 'Just a minute, I think we can do something about that.' He stretched to one side and clutched a large canvas haversack. After rummaging through it, he drew out a dog collar. 'There — what d'you think of that?'

The pup sniffed the well-worn leather. 'Had it in here for years,' reminisced the man. 'Come to think of it, the faithful old chap it first belonged to was a bit like you at your age. We shared a little place together not far from here. Had to have him put to sleep in the end — if you'll pardon the expression. Distemper. It was the kindest thing. Couldn't let the poor old fella suffer, could I? You do understand?'

He looked very sad and turned yet again to the bottle for consolation. 'And then, of course, there was the last dog who wore this collar. A labrador. A truly remarkable character that one. I could tell you quite a story about him.' The pup pushed its head under the man's arm. 'Like to hear it would you?' He eased the dog onto his lap.

'It was five years ago — the year my third wife left me. We lived in a cottage out of town then and the folks next door had a collie bitch. A beauty she was. Enough to turn any dog's head.

'Now, I don't know if animals can actually fall in love. Don't suppose anyone does for that matter. But if they can then, without doubt, that's what happened to those two. Of course, little friend, you may be a bit young to understand about things like that.' He winked and ruffled the pup's throat. 'Anyway, they were inseparable.

'But there was more to it than that . . . much more. Something a mere human like me could never explain. They each seemed to possess a remarkable gift for always knowing exactly what the other was doing. For instance, they'd scratch to leave their homes at precisely the same time. If I took the labrador for a walk — no matter how far — the collie would pester her owner to take her out too. And she'd drag her lead like a bloodhound straight to where we were. If the collie was ill, my dog would howl all day long. Quite incredible it was. Some sort of mental telepathy I suppose you'd call it.

'So you can imagine how sorry I was for them both when the people next door told me they were going to live twenty miles away. I knew that love-sick labrador would be heartbroken. But, of course, there was nothing I could do, was there?' He had another drink. 'Ah, that's better. It's thirsty work telling stories. Now where was I? Ah yes, the day they moved . . .

'Well, both of them were in a terrible state, I can tell you. Mine fought like a tiger to get out when the removal van left. And I could hear the bitch howling her pretty head off inside her owners' car. They had a real old tussle with her.

'For the rest of the week the labrador lay at our back door whining. Hour after hour it went on. He wouldn't eat, couldn't sleep. I don't think I've ever seen an animal suffer like he did. It was pitiful to watch, it really was.

'And then, suddenly one morning, he'd gone. The kitchen window was unlatched and somehow he'd managed to force it open. My wife told me she'd heard scraping noises in the night but thought nothing of it. However she did notice the time. It was three o'clock.

'Now, here's the uncanny part. I discovered later from the collie's owner that, at precisely three o'clock that same morning, a policeman saw the bitch vaulting over their garden fence. She had broken loose from her kennel.' The man hesitated as if expecting some reaction from the pup, and then carried on with his story.

'I wish I could tell you a happy ending, but I'm afraid their wasn't one. You see, later that day they found the dogs. Oh yes, they were together again. Lying side by side on a railway line. They'd both been hit by a train. And would you believe it, the spot was exactly half way between their two homes. In fact they're still there to this day. They always will be. We buried them in the same grave at the side of the track.' There were tears in the man's eyes now. 'Makes you think, little friend, doesn't it?

'Anyway,' he sniffed, '. . . to get back to you . . .' He looked at the black leather collar. There was a thin metal disc dangling from it. He gripped this between his fingers and held it in front of the pup's face. 'See the name on it? *Scruffy.* That's what I called both my dogs. Reckon it suits you, too.'

He fastened the collar round the pup's skinny neck and swayed back to inspect it. It looked more like a scarf. 'Mm — a bit on the generous side, but that won't matter.' He then carefully tilted a few drops of whisky onto his fingertips and sprinkled it over the pup's furry head. 'There,' he said solemnly. 'I hereby christen you Scruffy.'

The little dog placed a paw on the man's knee, lashing its tail until it almost flew off its bottom. The man gripped the paw and shook it. 'Sorry we can't have an address inscribed on it too. I mean we haven't really got one, have we? Unless it's "underneath the arches".'

With a quick tilt of his head he finished off the bottle of whisky. 'Ah well, I think it's time we both got some shut-eye. I'm sure you've had a hard day, and there's plenty to do tomorrow. But it's nice to have someone to talk to again.' With that they snuggled together under the blankets in the soothing glow of distant street lamps. And, lulled by the aroma of those magnificent feet, Scruffy the Third slept more blissfully than she'd ever done before...

10

Joseph P. Tibbles was awakened early, which was unusual. He was getting his face washed too, which was even more unusual. 'Good grief, little friend,' he spluttered as the pup licked away at his stubbly chin like a child with an iced lolly, '. . . it's barely daylight.'

He yawned and groped for the whisky bottle. 'Ugh,' he moaned, tipping it upside down. 'Empty.' He tapped the pup's nose with a fingertip. 'Now listen to me. The advantage of being an outcast from society is that one is also exempt from its tedious rules and regulations. We are unfettered by time and responsibility. We do not have to stampede through the streets at such unearthly hours with the common herd. We, my impetuous little friend, can lie in as long as we like. Now — go to sleep.'

But Scruffy persisted. She was hungry and he had access to cheese sandwiches and such things.

'All right, all right — you win,' he smiled, drying his face on his sleeve. 'But it's a bit early to start the rounds. No use trying to soft-soap housewives before their husbands have left for work. I found that out a long time ago.'

Scruffy wagged her tail and sat up. It was such a cosy feeling having a human around. She started grooming herself, wondering why he didn't do the same. The man watched her and noticed the scar on her leg as she tended it with her tongue. 'Been in the wars, have we?' he asked with compassion. 'Let's have a look. Mm — nasty. Still sore is it? Never mind, keep licking — that's the best thing to do.' He folded the blankets tight and rammed them inside the haversack. 'Right,' he commanded, 'let's see what providence has in store.'

He marched down the cinder road and turned off along pavements already hustling with red-nosed office workers. Scruffy panted close to the man's heels, occasionally yelping him to slow down when the pace became too brisk for her injured leg. Eventually the crowds petered out as they moved through broad boulevards flanked by large detached houses. 'This is it,' he announced. 'The land of plenty.' He patted the pup's head. 'Let's hope the natives are friendly. Here we go. And don't forget to limp. That sort of thing works wonders.'

A bonny woman in a quilted dressing gown answered the door of the first house they visited. 'Oh it's you again, is it?' she moaned as a biting gust of wind made her shiver. The man was unperturbed. He raised his trilby and gave her a sweeping bow. 'It *is* madam. Joseph P. Tibbles — at your service.' He glanced at Scruffy. 'And — er — my new associate.' The woman's stern expression melted. 'Really Mr. Tibbles, what will you think of next? I've no jobs for you today, but just a minute.' The man hummed confidently as she bounced off to the kitchen. 'Here,' she said when she returned, 'now I don't want to see you again for at least a week.' She gave him two parcels. 'The small one's for your associate — you old villain.'

Tibbles stepped back. 'Madam, you are most generous. In the words of Shakespeare — "For your great graces heaped upon me, poor undeserved, I can nothing render but allegiant thanks!" '

'Macbeth, Mr. Tibbles?'

'No madam, Henry VIII, Act Three.'

She pouted and shut the door. 'One of these days she'll guess right,' he grinned, tearing open a corner of the larger parcel. His face fell. 'Oh no — not cheese again!'

It was midday before they'd finished their calls, by which time Scruffy was quite worn out. The man's doorstep technique had been superb. 'Mm, now let's see,' he ruminated on their way back to town. 'There's some cold lamb, two cans of baked beans, half a loaf and more than a pound in cash. Oh yes, and those blooming cheese sandwiches. We shall dine well this day Scruffy.'

They made one more call on the way back, and it took considerably longer than the others. Two hours in fact. The man didn't knock or ring a bell this time. He just walked straight in. Scruffy sniffed. It smelled like the bottle he kept under the blankets. The man opened the smaller parcel and laid it under one of a number of round wooden tables dotted about the room. 'Here,' he beamed, 'we're lunching out today, little friend.' The pup wolfed down the tasty scraps of meat as the man walked over to a long shiny counter.

'Have a good morning did you Joseph?' A fat young woman with long strawy hair was pouring something into a glass. 'Yes my dear, quite rewarding — thanks to my partner over there.'

She strained her ample bosom across the counter. 'Aah, bless it. I'll bet that one tugged a few heartstrings. Wherever did you get it?'

'It limped into my worthless life yesterday evening Agnes, and I rather think it's here to stay. Appealing little chap, wouldn't you say?' She dipped into a large cardboard box and tossed him a packet of potato crisps. 'Here, give it these — they're on the house.'

The man's glass was refilled many times as Scruffy dozed contentedly under the table. When they left, she noticed he had developed a limp rather like her own. He seemed quite sleepy too, and his words were slurred.

They spent the rest of the afternoon beneath the railway arch. When the man slept, so did the pup. When he felt like talking she listened. For, though she may not have understood what he was saying, she could interpret his mood, and that's what really mattered. He was talking now as he sat the pup on his knee facing him, and the tone of his voice made her tail wag. '"New hatched, unfledged comrade . . . Thou and I am one . . . Co-mates in exile." Shakespeare, little friend. It's from Hamlet and As You Like It. That's exactly what we are, isn't it? We'll make a good team.'

He took a paper bag from his haversack and shared out the pieces of cold lamb given them that morning. 'And now,' he said, dusting himself down, 'it's time to be on the move again. I'm playing the Palace tonight. Hamlet. That always pulls 'em in. Come on — stay close. And remember — play up the limp like a good little trouper.'

Scruffy followed obediently. It was dark and the streetlamps sprinkled the frosty pavements with stars. It was quite a long walk before they arrived at a large, brightly-lit building where a long queue of people, muffled to the ears, jostled alongside the wall blowing into their hands. 'My public,' Tibbles said loftily. 'Now, watch this . . .'

The next moment he was sweeping back and forth

along the pavement addressing the astonished gathering in a booming voice. Scruffy did her best to stay with him, but finally gave up and lolled on the kerb, head in paws, watching in awe like the rest.

'To be, or not to be,' he roared, *'— that is the question:*

'Whether 'tis nobler in the mind to suffer
'The slings and arrows of outrageous fortune,
'Or to take arms against a sea of troubles . . .'

He lashed the air, crushed his trilby to his heaving breast and generally drove himself into such a frenzy that the mortified little dog suddenly lifted her head and howled in anguish like a foghorn. The crowd tittered. Then it chortled. Finally it almost collapsed in an explosion of belly-laughs and applause that could be heard half way down the street.

A coin clinked onto the kerb at Scruffy's feet. Then another and another. The man scooped them up and, with the pup hobbling at his heels, hurried along the queue muttering his astonished appreciation as more donations jingled about in his hat. A distinguished-looking gentleman patted his shoulder as he passed. 'A great act, old boy. Must have taken years to train that dog of yours. The timing was perfect.' Another gripped his arm. 'Funniest thing I've seen in ages.'

The big glass doors of the building swung open and the crowd, still chuckling, shuffled inside. Tibbles gaped into his trilby, now heavy with small change. 'Astounding,' he said at last, '...utterly astounding. Forty years in showbusiness and upstaged by a dog.' He bent down and swept the bewildered pup into his arms. 'Little friend,' he cried, 'you're a born artiste. If you can do that every night we'll make a fortune.' He kissed the top of her head and grasped a paw.

'Shake partner.' he grinned, 'I think we're in business.'

They called to see Agnes on their way back. 'Evening Joseph,' she chirped, 'a customer tells me that dog of yours brought the house down at the Palace tonight.' He patted Scruffy. 'Yes my dear — you might say we were a howling success.'

'Making the little chap a regular part of the act, are you?'

'Of course Agnes, of course. From now on we're a double. One cannot ignore such natural virtuosity. A large one please — and a bowl of milk for my partner.' He flung a fistful of silver on the counter. '. . . And take a gin for yourself.'

'My, you have hit the jack-pot haven't you?' she tittered. 'Here doggy — catch!' She dropped a packet of crisps over the counter. Scruffy nipped them up and carried them under the table she'd used earlier in the day. It was obviously going to be a long wait so she reckoned she might as well make herself comfy.

An hour or so later Agnes rang a bell and Joseph Tibbles stuffed a bottle down his coat. Scruffy stretched and toddled at his heel as he strode out into the night. Back under the railway arch the pup curled on his lap and he covered them both with the blankets. 'Aah,' he yawned, '— it's been quite a day. Think we deserve a lie in tomorrow. Goodnight Scruffy. Sleep well.'

Joseph Tibbles himself certainly slept well, refusing to budge until ten o'clock next morning despite his associate's feverish attentions since dawn. After a disgruntled breakfast of cheese sandwiches, he addressed the pup in very business-like terms.

'A-hem,' he began. 'I have given considerable and

earnest thought to your theatrical debut, little friend, and I have decided that the hours normally spent currying the favours of artless suburban housewives should in future be devoted to more Thespian pursuits. In other words, Scruffy — we shall start regular rehearsals forthwith.'

He stood up, bowed to the brick wall, and commenced: *'To be or not to be, — that is the question . . .'* The pup scratched herself. *'Whether 'tis nobler in the mind to suffer the slings and arrows of outrageous fortune . . .'* The pup turned away and nibbled the last cheese sandwich. '. . . *Or to take arms against a sea of troubles . . .'* The pup ambled along the wall, crouched down and piddled. Joseph P. Tibbles was scandalised.

He tried again but still made no impression. Finally he went through the routine exactly as he had done outside the Palace the night before, with all the melodramatic gestures. That did it. Right on cue the pup gave a howl that echoed through the arches like the siren of the London to Glasgow express. Her companion was ecstatic. 'That's it!' he cried triumphantly, '. . . it's not the immortal work of Shakespeare that does it — it's the Tibbles interpretation. Thank you, little friend, for such an inspiring accolade.'

Rehearsals went on all morning until Tibbles found that he could induce Scruffy to howl at will. He had only to clutch his breast and raise his voice to a particular pitch for the pup to instantly wail like a banshee. He went through his entire repertoire, prompting her to join in whenever he considered it most appropriate.

That evening at the Palace their performance caused a sensation — not merely with the queueing patrons but also with scores of passers-by who crowded round to listen. When they finally trotted back home, via Agnes's place, there was more money in the Tibbles' trilby than it had ever held before.

11

Life with Joseph Tibbles offered the one thing Scruffy cherished above all else . . . lasting human companionship. He made her feel wanted, and in return she gave him total and unquestioning loyalty.

But as the weeks went by she noticed a gradual change in him. His breathing became croaky and irregular. He was eating less — although he still made sure the pup had plenty and could now afford to buy her fresh meat each day. He was sleeping longer and some mornings Scruffy had difficulty rousing him at all. The trips to Agnes's were becoming more frequent, too.

One evening he knotted a thin rope to the pup's collar. 'Forgive me, little friend,' he said sadly, 'but my eyesight doesn't seem to be quite what it was. Things tend to get a little misty these days. It's just a precaution. I don't want to lose you. You *do* understand?' Scruffy didn't mind. She just felt more attached to him than ever.

She could sense what he wanted her to do and, when it was time, she led him along the cinder road and headed for the theatre. Traffic was no problem to her any more as she weaved through the noisy streets.

But it wasn't a good performance that night. In fact Joseph P. Tibbles flopped. The magic had gone. He forgot his lines. There was no flair and no frenzy

— just a tired, uninspiring recital in monotones that gave the pup no cues at all. Nobody applauded and only a few grudging coppers dropped into the trilby hat.

Scruffy pulled on the rope and urged him away, limping off in the direction of Agnes's place where she guessed he'd want to go. When he propped himself against the counter, the dog stayed at his feet instead of taking her usual position under the table. Agnes shook the actor's wrist. 'Joseph,' she frowned, 'are you all right?' He perked up when she pushed him a glass. 'Yes, yes, my dear. A little weary perhaps, nothing more.'

'But you look terrible.'

'Pressure, Agnes, pressure. Success in the theatre can be very demanding at times. Might have to take a short vacation.'

His hand shook as he drank and she watched him sadly. 'Yes, I think you should, Joseph. You've been looking groggy for a week or two. You mustn't do too much, you know. Got to take things easy at your age. You're no chicken.'

Scruffy eyed her master anxiously for the rest of the evening, ears alert for the tinkle of Agnes's bell that, it seemed, would never come. The instant she heard it she was on her feet and pulling him towards the door. 'Just a minute little friend, just a minute, I haven't picked up my night-cap yet.' Agnes handed him a bottle with obvious reluctance. 'You sure you want this tonight, Joseph?'

'More than ever,' he replied softly. 'Good-bye my dear.' She leaned over the counter. 'Here, Scruffy — your crisps,' she said. 'Take care of him, won't you.'

When they got back to the railway arch, Joseph Tibbles slid straight under the blankets. There were no bedtime stories. Just a short quotation that was barely audible. *'Death rock me to sleep, abridge my doleful days,'* he mumbled. '. . . Henry IV, Act Two, Scene Four. Goodnight little friend . . .'

When Scruffy tried to lick Joseph Tibbles awake the next morning, his face was colder than the brick wall at his back. She tugged his frayed sleeve and burrowed under his legs, but he didn't move. Then she crawled onto his chest and lay there for a long time peering into his wrinkled white face. When she nudged his hand with her wet nose it fell limply to the ground.

All that day she lay at his side whining softly. He'd never slept so long before. When evening came she barked to tell him it was time to go to Agnes's place, but he didn't seem to hear her. When she felt hungry she dragged the haversack across to him, waiting to be fed. But she had to eat alone.

It was the following afternoon when the policemen came. Scruffy snarled and stood rigid with her back against the actor's body. 'He's over there by the wall, sergeant — where the barmaid said we might find him. She's right, he certainly looks in a bad way.'

'Ah yes. See if you can get that dog out of the way.'

'It doesn't look too friendly.'

'No it doesn't. Just a minute.' The sergeant dropped to one knee. 'Come on then laddie — you've done your bit. We'll take over now.' Scruffy wasn't sure what to do. Perhaps they'd know how to wake him up. She hobbled to the officer who picked up the rope lead. When he shook Joseph Tibbles's shoulders they slid sideways along the wall. The sergeant pressed his palm against the actor's chest and shook his head slowly. 'He's a goner all right. Probably been dead for some time. Poor old stick. Better call an ambulance. Come on, there's nothing more *we* can do.'

'What about the dog?'

'Probably lives around here somewhere. It's got a collar. I should leave it. We'll check later, if it's still here we'll take it in.' The other spotted something and turned back. 'No point in leaving this, sergeant,' he called. 'Look, it's a full bottle of Scotch.'

Scruffy lay across the body until the ambulance arrived. The driver drew the pup away by her lead and two white-coated attendants rolled Joseph Tibbles onto a stretcher and slotted it into the rear of the vehicle. Scruffy yelped and broke away as the twin doors crashed shut. 'Sorry mate,' said one of the attendants, 'you're wasting your time. He's not coming back.'

The dog flung herself against the doors, raking them with her claws as the ambulance slowly moved off along the cinder road. As it nosed into the traffic stream she careered after it, barking. The ambulance accelerated, edging passed the slow-moving inside lane. Scruffy leapt forward, the rope lead whipping behind, missing the murderous wheels of a heavy lorry by inches. But she didn't even notice them. She was blind to everything but those white shiny doors now pulling further away.

Dodging between both lanes, she chased the ambulance as fast and as far as she could. Heaving herself to the kerb she stared at the ambulance as it swung out of sight round a corner. She stayed where she was for a moment or two then forced herself to her throbbing legs and staggered defiantly on in the same direction.

There was no sign of the ambulance now. But, as

she was about to turn back, she spotted it again. It was parked in a short line of vehicles waiting to cross a river bridge. She tried to run but her legs refused to respond and she crashed to her side panting huskily.

Still she refused to give in, crawling forward a few painful movements at a time. The traffic began to stir again, but very slowly and Scruffy struggled on gaining fractionally all the time. With only a dozen yards to go, a man carrying a red and white sign stepped briskly between the vehicles and they juddered to a halt. The ambulance, however, had already passed him and was on its way over the bridge. Scruffy started to follow it, but the man hopped sideways and stamped on the dog's lead jerking her backwards. 'And where d'you think you're going?' he thundered. 'See this?' He jabbed a grubby finger at the sign. 'It says *stop.* And that means dogs too. Understand? Now get off with you.'

Scruffy cringed as he drew back his boot. A car horn shrieked and the terrified dog threw herself between some iron railings at the roadside. She yelped as she tumbled headlong down a steep bank and, seconds later, icy water exploded about her. She flayed her legs in panic and felt herself drifting slowly under the bridge. As she did so, the loop at the end of her thin rope lead hooked over a bent nail in a wooden mooring post that jutted out of the water. Scruffy paddled her front legs trying desperately to reach the bank. With her paws clawing the air only inches from it, the rope tautened and grabbed her back. Her hind quarters sank but her feet found the hard face of a large stone embedded in the shallow muddy bed of the river's edge. By straining her back legs she was able to thrust against her tethered collar, keeping her head above the water.

A gusty wind puckered the surface and thick grey scum flowed over her like molten lava. Her injured leg gave way and skidded off the submerged stone as she lashed the water, coughing out vile-tasting mouthfuls. Her back legs retrieved their foothold on the stone and she lunged forward into her collar again, sucking frantic gulps of air.

It was then Scruffy spotted the bull terrier. She choked out a succession of urgent barks and he ambled nearer. When he drew level he sat down and watched. She gave a long, plaintive howl and thrashed the water again. The bull terrier shied away as cold spray flicked across his impassive face. Then, as if he had suddenly grasped the full drama of the situation, he leapt through the air, his body thwacking the surface alongside Scruffy and creating a tidal wave that swept her from her foothold.

The terrier paddled hard to keep afloat as his powerful jaws scooped up the lead, grinding the soaked fibres between his teeth. Scruffy felt her hind legs sink into the mud and the murky water lapped her chin. The other dog gnawed madly at the rope. Scruffy sank deeper. Her head fell back and slowly disappeared as water surged into her lungs.

The bull terrier rammed his stocky forelegs against the mooring post and heaved with all his strength, shaking the half-chewed rope in fury. A few seconds later he was lurching backwards through the water as the fibres ripped apart. The dog then lunged forward again, snapping up the shortened lead still attached to Scruffy's collar and scrambled with it to the bank. Once on solid ground he reared his thick muscular neck, inching back, body hugging the earth, until the bitch's hind legs squelched out of the river bed and her lolling head emerged above the surface. A few more mighty tugs and she was sprawling on the bank like a wet mop.

The exhausted bull terrier shook himself and dropped down at her side, shivering and panting, watching the lifeless young bitch with half-closed eyes. Then he stood up and sniffed her from head to tail, gently prodding her with his paw. She shuddered and lay still again. The other dog gave a deep, guttural bark and nudged her with his short muzzle. She coughed, making him prick his ears. He stepped back, watching her struggle for breath. A gush of water spurted from her limp mouth and trickled over the edge of the river bank as her body writhed on the ground.

After a while she breathed more easily and flickered open her eyes. Everything was hazy and confused. Then she gradually focused them on the rugged bull terrier at her side.

Scruffy had seen nothing quite like him before, standing there square-shouldered and steel-limbed, his smooth brindled coat close-cropped and glistening wet, stretched tight over a solid frame. The neck was strong and beautiful, bulging with hard, flexing muscle; the white chest wide; the well-rounded rib-cage looking as impregnable as a metal grill, narrowing to his flat, taut belly. She gazed at his noble head with its deep-set eyes, and those magnificent jaws that had saved her life . . . wide and efficient as a bear-trap. Everything about him suggested courage, tenacity and swashbuckling self-assurance. In short, he was a truly splendid animal.

Scruffy tried to stand but her legs collapsed. The bull terrier stretched alongside her as if to convince her there was no hurry. She licked his spear-shaped ear and this thin tail drummed the ground. Then, very timorously, he nosed his way round and sniffed her rear end . . . which may not seem a particularly chivalrous gesture to a human, but to him it was like stealing a fleeting kiss in the moonlight.

They stayed together until Scruffy felt strong enough to move. The terrier watched her climb shakily to her feet. She swayed and he waited at her shoulder until she regained her balance. He walked a short way along the bank then turned and barked softly, pressing her to follow. She approached unsteadily, one feeble step at a time. He moved on a little further, again barking encouragement.

They continued in this manner until the terrier began climbing a flight of wooden steps leading up the river bank. Scruffy lay at the foot. He turned, gripped her short lead in his teeth, and crawled up backwards, hauling the panting bitch from one step to the next until they reached the top. He let her rest a while before setting off along the pavement, glancing back every few yards to make sure she was following.

Some fifteen minutes later Scruffy stopped and thrust her quivering nose in the air. She panted excitedly and turned into a narrow cinder road. The terrier watched, barking her to return, but this time she ignored him. He snarled impatiently and waited, treading the pavement. This was just like a bitch, utterly unpredictable! When he eventually followed, he found her lying in the shadow of a railway arch. She was on an old grey blanket and was licking a canvas haversack propped against the brick wall.

For a long time the bull terrier stood perfectly still cocking his elegant head, but she didn't seem to notice him now. He barked once more, then turned and walked slowly back up the cinder road. Scruffy heard the soft munch of his paws and gazed after him. She wanted to follow, but the blanket and the familiar smells that reminded her of Joseph Tibbles, held her back.

The terrier stopped half-way along the road and swung round to face her, growling his disapproval. Scruffy instinctively moved forwards, but gave a flurried whimper and rolled back onto the blanket When she looked again he was disappearing round the corner. She trembled. A strange compelling urge she had never felt before made her leap to her feet. She hesitated a moment longer to stare back into the railway arch, then limped off as fast as she could along the cinder road.

12

'Hi there, Butch — who's your friend? Haven't seen *that* one before. Showing it the ropes are you, you young scrounger?'

The bull terrier rubbed his rippling shoulders against the elderly newspaper-seller's legs, glancing back at Scruffy who had sidled into a shop doorway.

'Timid little blighter, isn't it?' Butch shuffled his bottom on the pavement as the man pulled a handful of dog biscuits from his pocket. 'Hey there,' he called to Scruffy, 'are you watching closely? See the routine? This fella's an artiste, I'll tell you.'

The man gave Butch a second helping. This time the dog gathered the biscuits loosely in his jaws and carried them to the doorway, where he dropped them at Scruffy's feet. The man gaped and slapped his cheek. 'Blimey — I don't believe it,' he cried. 'You're actually giving food away. What's the matter Butch? Gone all soft, have you?' He thought for a moment. 'Ah — I get it now. She's a girl dog isn't she? Yes, that's what it is.' He roared with husky laughter. 'Looks as though she's got you under her paw already. Serves you right, you cocky young rascal.'

As Scruffy munched the biscuits Butch hopefully returned for more, but the man waved him away. 'Oh no . . . that's it for today,' he chortled. 'If you're hen-pecked enough to give her half your earnings, that's just too bad.'

The bull terrier strutted off, confidently dodging the traffic. The bitch had no idea where he was leading her, but she felt safe hobbling along by his side. He turned off the road into a narrow cobbled passage between the shops. Ahead of them was a large patch of open ground littered with battered motor cars. It was like a traffic cop's nightmare . . . as though every driver in town had tried to beat the lights at the same time. The bull terrier picked his way through the debris. When Scruffy hesitated, he turned back and gave her lead a tug. Eventually he stopped next to a large blue saloon, sniffed one of its tyreless wheels and cocked his back leg against it.

The doors hung limply on rusty hinges. Butch gripped his companion's lead again and hopped through a rear one, but she thrust her front paws against the sill. He dropped the lead, leapt onto a black leather bench seat and lay panting with his chin over the edge. Scruffy pushed her head through the door and sniffed. The terrier hadn't been the only occupant. There was a profusion of doggy smells in there, all quite inviting. There was carpet on the floor, threadbare but homely, and the seat looked cosy, despite tufts of stuffing sprouting through like tumbleweed. She crawled in, glanced coyly at Butch, and eased herself onto the seat by his side, draping her throat over his smooth shoulders and dozing off.

The nap was short and sweet. Suddenly something crashed against the side of the dilapidated car and Scruffy's hackles rose when two enormous paws thumped the window. Gaping jaws grinned at her as the evening sunlight flashed across long pointed fangs. She shuddered. It was like staring into a cave full of stalagmites and stalactites. A moment later a fawn Alsatian lolloped inside, tilting the rickety car with a tinny groan.

Scruffy scrambled over Butch as the intruder began to sniff her feverishly, wafting its bushy tail. The little bitch peeled back her lips and snarled. The nerve of the brute! The Alsatian recoiled, blinking its big brown eyes. It looked most aggrieved at her rejection.

Until now Butch had done nothing except watch the ritual with one eye. He obviously considered the newcomer harmless enough. But, as it made further attempts to philander with his little ward, his spine arched and he growled menacingly. The effect was instant. The Alsatian gave a disgruntled whimper, skulking out through the rear door and in again through the front one. There it thudded its huge frame into one of the bucket seats, drooping its head over the back and eyeing Butch with pained reproach. Scruffy moved closer to the bull terrier. She was most impressed. He'd certainly put that canine Casanova in its place.

It was obvious however, that the Alsatian was no stranger and, judging by the way it made itself at home, Scruffy could only assume they must have shared the tenancy of the wrecked car — Butch's territory being the rear half.

But things were not as clear cut as that. No sooner had she settled down again than the pointed snout of a black and white collie poked through the door. Scruffy blinked. Between its teeth was an old Wellington boot. It laid this gently on the ground and, with ears erect and tail held low, cautiously approached Scruffy. Their wet noses met. This one was a bitch. Butch bustled between them and the collie walked away, picking up her black rubber boot and hauling it past the Alsatian to take her place on the seat next to him. Here she did an extraordinary thing. She wrapped her shaggy body round the Wellington and began to lick it lovingly — just as a mother might have tended her own pup. Then she stretched down and dragged from the floor a piece of frayed blanket, which she spread over the boot. The Alsatian watched compassionately as if he understood.

It was dusk when the next tenant scrambled in through the rear door. It tripped and fell flat on its face, splattering over the floor a soggy meat pie that had been jammed in its mouth. Scruffy's nostrils tremored, then she wagged her tail. There was a familiar aura about it. Like Joseph Tibbles when he'd been to Agnes's place.

The dog tried to stand but its legs gave way and it sprawled in a heap on the floor where it seemed content to stay — looking up at Scruffy with a bilious expression. It was just about the oddest-looking hound she could have imagined . . . wrinkled and droopy, with thick bow legs and Charlie Chaplin feet. It was cross-eyed and mangy, with a face like rucked-up carpet. But then she'd never before met a boxer that had gone to seed. Butch watched disdainfully as it closed its eyes and sank into oblivion with a grating, deep-throated snore that seemed to drill right through Scruffy's ear-drums. She sighed. Surely there couldn't be any more of them. But there was.

She saw it emerge through the gloom like a broom-head with legs. It was bandy and so low-slung that the long grey hair on its back barely cleared the ground. Yet, despite its diminutiveness, the cairn terrier approached with the arrogance of a game-cock. The instant it spotted Scruffy it froze — small pointed ears jutting forward, dark hazel eyes narrowing in distrust beneath shaggy eyebrows, and its thin black lips tightened in anger. Butch showed far more concern about this one's arrival than any of the others. He stepped in front of Scruffy and planted his feet firmly on the edge of the seat, growling and staring straight into the cairn's shifty eyes as if to say: 'Just try something, that's all.'

It heaved onto the back seat and crouched. Then, suddenly, it sprang snake-like at Butch's throat. The bull terrier didn't flinch. He simply cuffed the cairn in mid-flight with his powerful paw, knocking it sideways onto the floor. Scruffy was astounded. The cheek of it! She was certain her hero could have torn it apart if he'd wished. But Butch knew he'd done enough to show who was boss, as the other climbed back onto the seat and curled up, cursing under his breath in ill-tempered snarls.

The other animals paid no attention to the brief skirmish. It was a regular occurrence. The cairn was notorious. It spent most days wandering alone, squaring up to anything on four legs, no matter how formidable, and the flesh beneath its matted hair was battle-scarred to glory. It wasn't a thoroughbred cairn. Its grooming and temperament indicated perhaps a cross between a water rat and a praying mantis. Only Butch, it appeared, could handle the little rebel.

In fact, as Scruffy gazed at the noble bull terrier, she was convinced he could handle anything. He was obviously a born leader — indifferent to fear yet tolerant and considerate. There was no doubt that among this strange little band of dogs, his bark was law. They respected his rugged dignity. As with all leaders of packs, his authority to guide, protect and punish was unquestionable.

None of this was surprising. Butch's courage was deeply bred. More than a century ago his tenacious ancestors had been trained to shrug off the most appalling injuries in public dog-fights — those outrageous and bloody spectacles in which the contestants battled like gladiators for up to six murderous hours. Bull terriers were chosen for this ruthless sport as a breed that would accept defeat only in death, despite broken backs, shattered limbs and the most terrible atrocities.

Butch had exhibited these qualities before the rest of the group many times. None of them, for instance, would ever forget the time he was hit by a car. He'd simply shaken himself and strolled off without a murmur, leaving the rueful motorist inspecting a dented metal grille and shattered headlight. Scruffy nestled close to him.

The collie bitch cuddled her Wellington boot as the Alsatian ruffled her fur with a weary sigh. The cairn cursed softly and the punch-drunk boxer on the floor twitched and rolled its bloodshot eyes. And, by the light of the yellow moon streaming through the derelict family saloon, they all settled down for the night.

None of the gang heard Scruffy slink away during the night. When Butch realised she'd gone he searched every car in the dump. The others watched him with mild curiosity. It slowly dawned on the Alsatian that the loss of a female was well worth a sniff or two and it bounded out of the car to join its leader. A few minutes later it was loping after Butch as he headed off along the main street, pausing every now and then to snuffle the pavement.

The Alsatian watched the bull terrier turn into the cinder road that led under the railway arch. The bitch was lying face down on Joseph Tibbles's blankets. As Butch approached she looked up with melancholic eyes. He slunk beside her and licked her tenderly. This place had some deep significance. She was waiting for something or someone — that much Butch could sense. But there was no way she could tell him about it, so there seemed no way he could help. The sudden rumble of a train passing overhead made the watching Alsatian jump and rush back along the cinder road. Butch was imperturbable as ever.

Scruffy was glad he had come for her. If he hadn't, she would have stayed. But, when he got up and walked away barking her to follow, she obeyed and accompanied him back along the road to where the Alsatian was waiting. She would return, of course. She had to. If Joseph Tibbles showed up he'd want her to be there.

The Alsatian lashed its tail and sniffed her. Butch gave her a reassuring look that told her he'd order the other dog away if she wanted him to. But she didn't bother. The soppy brute was quite inoffensive really. It was just his way. So she let him sniff a while and then the three of them trotted off along the empty street.

Butch called to see the old newspaper seller on the way. 'Still around is she Butch?' he greeted, handing out the biscuits. 'I'd keep an eye on that Alsatian though if I were you. You know what he's like with the girls.'

At the sight of a burly policeman crossing the street, Butch gave a gruff warning and ushered the others away.

'Morning officer,' piped the news-seller peeling a paper from the bundle under his arm. 'My friends don't seem too keen on meeting you.' The other snorted: 'No, and I'm not surprised. I know that Alsatian.'

'You do . . . how's that?'

'Used to be one of us. His name's Sam.'

'I don't follow you.'

'Used to be in the force. He was a police dog.'

'What! That one a police dog! You must be joking. He's scared of his own shadow. A cat chased him the full length of the street the other day.'

The policeman sighed. 'Yes, I can believe it. That's the point. That's why he isn't with us any more.'

'What happened?'

'Oh, he was hopeless. Treated the whole business as a lark. Soft as toffee. Couldn't tell the cops from the robbers. Did the balmiest things.'

'Like what?'

The policeman looked sheepishly at his big black boots as if what he was about to say was going to cause himself acute embarrassment. But the other man egged him on. 'Well, I'll tell you why we finally got rid of him . . .

'He'd been sent with a police dog-handler to sniff out a buried hand grenade on a farm. It was a relic of the war. The area had been used as an Army firing range.

'Sam found it all right, so the officer took the pin out and slung the grenade as far as he could into an open field so it would explode in safety. This gormless animal does no more than leap over the fence, pick the blasted thing up in his teeth and bring it back. The handler almost fainted when Sam calmly dropped it at his feet and wagged his tail. Obviously the officer hared off down the lane. And what does Sam do? He charges after him with the blooming grenade in his mouth.'

'Crikey,' oggled the other man '. . . go on.'

'Well, it ended up with Sam pinning the terrified officer to a tree and dropping the grenade down the front of his tunic. Thank heavens it didn't go off. It was later found to be unserviceable. But the poor man was a nervous wreck for days and, as far as Sam was concerned, that was his lot. The superintendent was furious. "Get rid of that idiotic animal before it gets us all killed," he said.'

The news-seller nodded. 'Now I see what you mean.'

'Mind you,' went on the policeman. 'There'd been other incidents before that. One in particular. The sergeant nearly had a fit.'

'What was that?'

'Er — well, you know the dog's a bit of a lad with the ladies?'

'Yes, that's pretty obvious.'

'There was this time he was supposed to trace a missing criminal from the scent of a piece of the suspect's clothing. Sam had dragged his handler along a particular street and was throwing himself against one of the front doors. Barking and making a heck of a racket he was. A shifty-looking character came to the door and the officer arrested him on suspicion and carted him off to the station. Sam just sat there sniffing his trouser legs.

'The bloke was cursing and demanding to see a lawyer. But the officer told him: "this animal's a highly-trained tracker. It knows what it's doing." Then the man slapped the charge office table and roared: "Yes, it knew what it was doing all right. I'll tell you why it tried to batter my door down. It wasn't me it was after, you blithering idiot. It was my labrador bitch in the back kitchen. She's on heat — and that flamin' animal of yours knew it."

'After further inquiries it was obvious the man was innocent. He'd got a stone-wall alibi.'

Tears of laughter streamed down the news-seller's face. 'That's the daftest thing I've heard in years,' he spluttered, '. . . it really is. But what happened after Sam was discharged from the force? How did he end up on the streets?'

'As a matter of fact I did make a few inquiries. Apparently he was taken on by some security people as a guard dog at a warehouse in town.'

'That's a laugh.'

'Yes, he didn't last long there either. Seems some thieves broke in one night and fed him cans of meat while they loaded a lorry with portable radios. And, for good measure, they took Sam along too and later sold him to some unsuspecting old dear as a house dog. I was told he got a neighbour's pedigree show bitch into trouble. There was a big row about it. The woman must have slung Sam out soon after that. Don't know who owns him now — if anyone still does.'

The news-seller rubbed his chin. 'I think he's a mate of Butch's — the bull terrier you saw. There's a gang of them. I've no idea where they live, or how. I give them tit-bits. Suppose they must have other regular calls. They're a friendly bunch though. All except the bandy-legged cairn. That one's a villain.'

'Oh, why?'

'Never out of trouble. Always scrapping. Not much bigger than a rabbit but I've seen it tackle dogs ten times its own size. You don't often see it with the others. Seems to prefer going around on its own. That's why I call it Solo.'

'Solo — mm, I see. And where did he come from?'

'Oh he's been a stray for years. Someone told me he'd once landed his woman owner in court. She was sued by a local pigeon fancier. Seems the dog kept catching his birds. The chap told the magistrates that Solo was actually seen holding a pigeon down with one paw and digging a hole with the other. He swore the little sadist was trying to bury the poor thing alive.'

The policeman shuddered. 'Very friendly, I must say.'

'Yes. Anyway soon after that, to its owner's relief, it wandered off. Someone found it and took it back, but she went hysterical and refused to take it in again. No one'll go anywhere near it now.' The policeman patted the top of his helmet and strolled away. 'Ah well,' he sighed, 'it takes all sorts to make a world.'

13

For all members of the little gang the most important business of every day was filling stomachs. Each had their own haunts, though occasionally a couple might scavenge together. Not the cairn, of course. He was a loner.

His main diet was curried beef. This was because the only human friend he'd got was a cook at an Indian restaurant. For some unaccountable reason Solo transformed into a fussy, impeccably-behaved animal the instant they met. He called every lunch time at the back door of the restaurant, waiting patiently for the man to pat his scrubby head and talk to him in a sing-song voice. The helpings of curried beef were exorbitant — far more than Solo could ever eat. There was often enough to have fed half the gang. But he wasn't prepared to share his spoils with anyone.

Big Sam the Alsatian was less organised. He simply heaved over dustbins at random, scattering the contents on the ground and sorting out anything edible. He was very fond of fish and made a tour of predominantly Catholic areas every Friday night. Sometimes the collie bitch tagged along, trailing her Wellington boot.

The boxer's sole diet seemed to consist of stodgy meat pies.

On this mellow April morning, Butch and Scruffy would dine together . . . on chop suey. It was the bull terrier's favourite food. Unfortunately, unlike Solo, he had no friends in the catering trade, so it meant a furtive raid on one of the Chinese restaurants.

He parked Scruffy at the street corner and made a quick reconnoitre. There were some waste food bins in the yard at the back of the cafe. He barked and Scruffy joined him. Stretching on his back legs, he hooked his forepaws over the edge of a bin and toppled it over with a loud clatter.

Scruffy stiffened. With a blood-curdling cry, a man waving a meat cleaver crashed through a door. Butch's frantic bark shook Scruffy into action and they both shot off with the Chinese owner screaming on their tails.

As the man burst into the street he thudded straight into the arms of a passing policeman, knocking the wind clean out of him. His colleague, a sergeant, grabbed the man's collar and hauled him back. 'What the devil's going on, Mr. Wang,' he snapped good-naturedly. 'You can't go around chopping people's heads off.'

The furious Mr. Wang jabbered incoherently and pointed at the dogs, now skidding out of sight round a corner.

'There, there, calm down,' soothed the officer. 'You'll never catch them now. Been in the bins again, eh? Never mind, we'll keep an eye open in case they come back. But, for Pete's sake, go and put that blooming hatchet away — it gives me the willies.' Mr. Wang scowled and returned to the restaurant. The sergeant shrugged. 'Don't suppose they were doing any harm. The stuff only gets dumped anyway.' He gave the other officer a sinister look. 'Unless, of course, Mr. Wang was after the dogs for a *different* reason.'

'How d'you mean?' frowned his colleague.

'Well,' said the sergeant, straight-faced, 'there are some funny things being served up in restaurants these days — and meat isn't all that cheap.'

'You mean . . .' The other blinked, then grinned. 'Aw — give over, sergeant. You're pulling my leg, aren't you?'

There were plenty of other Chinese restaurants and Butch eventually got his chop suey. Scruffy wasn't too keen on it so he sorted her out some tasty scraps from the fish market across town.

By dusk they were back at their 'digs' on the wrecked car lot. Sam and the collie were already settled in the front of the saloon and the surly little Solo was propped in his allotted place at the back, cursing Sam whose soft eyes blinked at him from the gap between the bucket seats. He had no respect for the docile Alsatian. How could a hulking animal like that be so chicken-hearted? He was an insult to his breed. Look at those fangs. What Solo would have given for them! And the magnificent claws! But all the silly great goose ever did with those was scratch himself. Now, if only he, Solo, had been built like that. For one thing he'd have soon sorted out that high and mighty bull terrier.

He was shaken from his villainous musings when Butch thudded onto the rear seat, bouncing Solo straight to the floor. The cairn snapped the air and the straw-like fur along his spine stood on end. Butch ignored him so he took a swipe at Sam's nose instead and climbed back into his place.

It was dark now and Scruffy noticed Butch was getting restless. He kept pricking his ears and glancing anxiously at the door. Finally he jumped from the seat and hurried out into the night. Scruffy followed. At the end of the cobbled passage he turned, urging her to go back. But she limped defiantly to his side. He hesitated then plodded along the street.

A few minutes later he stopped outside a drab stone building. Scruffy sniffed. It smelt just like Agnes's place and thoughts of her beloved Joseph Tibbles flooded back. A sign over the entrance read 'The Prince of Denmark.' Butch sat on the doorstep.

Inside, spread-eagled like a bearskin rug in the crowded bar, was their colleague, the boxer. The place droned with the gruff voices of men in heavy tweeds with even heavier eyes, and everywhere reeked of beer fumes and stale tobacco. A jacketless man bursting through crimson braces lifted a draw-bridge style hatch in the long wooden counter and placed a half-filled pint glass on the floor. 'Come and get it, Hamlet,' he called. 'It's last orders.'

The cross-eyed boxer gave his tail a weary wag, heaved himself to his feet and immediately keeled over. A short thin man at the counter leaned forward, screwing up his eyes. 'Hey, landlord,' he muttered, 'I'll swear that animal's blotto.' The other nodded ruefully. 'That's right sir. Trouble is he never knows when he's had enough.'

'You mean he's often like that?'

'Most nights. Depends on how many of the regulars call in. They all know him. He drinks like a fish.'

The dog made another groggy attempt to stand, propping against the nearest customer's leg. Then, with his flat feet seemingly intent on taking different directions, he reeled across the floor and thrust his face against the rim of the pint glass, flicking at the dark-brown liquid inside with slow, deliberate laps of his yellow-coated tongue. 'Well, I'll be blowed,' puffed the thin man tilting his bowler to the back of his head.

'Oh that's nothing,' sighed the landlord. 'He once got locked in after closing time and fell asleep near the fire over there. The wife smelled something burning in the night. When I dashed downstairs there he was with the hair on his rump singed to blazes. He didn't even know he'd been on fire.'

A heavily-rouged barmaid wriggled through the hatch and started collecting glasses. She ruffled the boxer's ear as she passed. 'Poor old thing,' she cooed. 'It's a shame letting you get in such a state, it really is.'

'Oh he's all right,' assured the landlord, '. . . aren't you Hamlet?'

'Hamlet!' The thin man tapped his shoulder. 'That's an odd name for a dog. Who the devil christened it that?'

The other grinned. 'I did. The pub's called The Prince of Denmark, isn't it? Hamlet was Prince of Denmark, wasn't he? That dog's my most regular customer — so I've called him Hamlet. Appropriate, don't you think sir?'

The man eyed the bemused animal, now lying on its side, its crumpled snout overlapping the rim of the upturned beer glass. 'Ugh,' he grimmaced '. . . old Willie Shakespeare must be turning in his grave.'

Meanwhile, back on the doorstep, Butch was getting impatient. He growled angrily and leapt to his feet. Scruffy watched in trepidation as he shouldered open the bar door and stalked through barking like the Colt Forty-nine of a Dodge City gun-slinger. The landlord nudged the man at his elbow. 'Ah — here he comes. Wyatt Earp himself, right on time.'

'Blimey, not another,' gasped the thin man.

'Oh, he doesn't drink. He just comes to fetch Hamlet. Don't know where they go, but it's obvious that bull terrier's the boss. Watch . . .' The boxer struggled to his feet and headed for the door. 'See, what did I tell you. Reckon if it wasn't for that one, we'd never get Hamlet out of the place sometimes.'

The barmaid skipped across the room. 'Here you are, love,' she cried, stuffing a meat pie into the dog's mouth, '. . . got to have something on your stomach. See you tomorrow. Take care now.'

She might well have said that. Once outside, Hamlet lunged straight off the pavement and weaved across the busy road like a sailor on shore leave. Tyres squealed, but Hamlet must have had more lives than an alley-cat and somehow he manoeuvred through it all. In fact, to the astonishment of one white-faced motorist who had to stop dead, the pixillated hound calmly cocked his leg against one of the wheels and stood there piddling away his indulgence in the moonlight.

Once the three dogs were safely on the opposite pavement, Butch and Scruffy positioned themselves on either side of Hamlet and guided him back to the 'digs' — the bull terrier cuffing him every now and again with his paw. When they arrived, Sam and Solo were asleep, but the collie bitch was pacing anxiously outside the car. As Hamlet collapsed at her feet she wafted her tail and sniffed him with genuine concern. It was obvious the collie regarded him with affection, though Scruffy failed to see how any self-respecting bitch could fancy such an ugly, prune-faced creature.

Mind you, even she had to admit there was something oddly appealing about him. Perhaps it was because he looked so helpless lying there. Of course she wasn't to know that the collie remembered him before he started falling apart at the seams, as you might say. In those days he possessed many of Butch's superb qualities. He was graceful, poised and quick-witted — a fine figure of a dog. Now he had enough imperfections to give any show judge a heart attack. But the collie still stood by him.

Butch shook Hamlet by the scruff of the neck. He twitched a few times then pulled himself into the car. Now Scruffy understood why he'd never claimed one of the comfy seats. It was easier to simply pass out on the floor, which he now did.

The collie jumped into her place at the front. Scruffy watched her for a while, intrigued with her strange obsession over the Wellington boot. She noticed that all the others gave the object a wide berth and once when Sam inadvertently sat on it, she nipped his backside, making him yelp. It was quite apparent the collie regarded the boot as a living thing. This was because, for some reason, she had never been able to conceive her own pups — though, heaven help her, she was amiable enough at the right times. So, to her, the boot was the object upon which she was lavishing her suppressed maternal instincts, telling herself it needed her. That's why she would guard it with her life. No one could ever have convinced her there wasn't a small heart pumping away somewhere inside that Wellington.

There was something else Scruffy noticed about the collie. Sounds never seemed to distract her in any way and she was the only one of the group Butch never barked orders to. Instead he would nudge her or make some other significant gesture in the way dogs do when they want to communicate. In fact, it was

Scruffy and her pups

Butch

Solo

Collie

Sam

Hamlet

Today the Mirror chooses . . .

THE DOG OF THE YEAR

by JACK STONELEY

THE name is SCRUFFY. He was the lovable little mongrel in the TUESDAY cage who put a lump in the throat of the nation.

Tuesday was the day he arrived in the cage. Tuesday, a week later, was the day he was due to leave the cage—to die because no one wanted him.

YOU saved him from taking his last walk from the condemned cell. **YOU** refused to let Scruffy die.

It is ten weeks since Scruffy's pathetic eyes peered from the front page of the Daily Mirror—in the picture reproduced above. He was due to die that morning.

For days he had watched the good-looking dogs at Heartbreak House—the Manchester and District Home for Lost Dogs—taken out to freedom by visitors.

He didn't think he had a dog's chance. His legs were too long . . . his feet too big.

But, overnight, from being the pooch without a pal he became the most wanted dog in Britain.

NEVER before did one little mongrel have such an impact on the nation.

EVERYBODY WANTED HIM. Telephone lines were jammed with SOS (Save Our Scruffy) calls. People travelled miles to queue outside his cell in Heartbreak House.

SERVICES JOINED IN

Five hundred telegrams avalanched into the Dogs' Home and the Mirror offices. Lads in the Army, the Navy and the RAF joined in the fight to save him.

And when it was all over a kid called Derrick Davies, aged four, threw his chubby arms round Scruffy's neck and cried: "*Daddy—he's really mine.*"

Proudly, young Derrick led the tail-wagging mongrel out of the condemned cell to his home in Woodhouse Park, Manchester.

Once again Scruffy had a fireside to curl in front of. His own ball. A dish of his own. Someone to rub his ears and take him for walks.

"Scruffy's a grand little dog," said Derrick's mother last night, "and he just loves children."

THE soft eyes of Scruffy saved his pals, too. **By the Tuesday evening there wasn't an unwanted dog left at Heartbreak House. They, too, had found homes . . . thanks to the rush for Scruffy.**

So, who else for the Dog Of The Year but Scruffy—the pooch that touched ten thousand hearts?

● *Loved at last—Scruffy gets a hug from four-year-old Derrick Davies, the boy who led him home—from the condemned cell.*

TOMORROW: The Face of the Year

A *Daily Mirror* headline

Scruffy

because of this that she had become a stray. She began life as a sheepdog, but was thrown out by the farmer because she never responded to his whistles. He didn't realise why. She was stone deaf.

As Scruffy slid onto the rear seat next to Butch, she suddenly felt she knew them all so much better.

14

As the weeks of spring passed, Scruffy experienced a deepening sense of loyalty towards the motley band of outcasts and, being one of them, made her feel secure. Not that she ever forgot Joseph Tibbles. She still made daily pilgrimages to the railway arch. But, for the rest of the time, she was content to be at Butch's side, helping him whenever she could in his onerous responsibilities as a leader.

She found herself sharing his concern for them all and was restless as a mother hen at night until each roost in the rusty old motor car was occupied.

Hamlet was a constant source of anxiety. He was even trundling off to the Prince of Denmark hours before opening time, happy to doze on the doorstep until the landlord let him in. Each evening either Scruffy or the faithful collie would help Butch escort him home.

Sam too was a problem. Complaints by bitch owners about his amorous rampages through a nearby housing estate made him a 'wanted' dog — especially as he usually knocked over their dustbins at the same time.

Scruffy found herself even showing concern over the incorrigible Solo and spent frantic hours searching town for the little blackguard when he once went missing for three days. He'd been rat-hunting and had chased one into an open drain where he became trapped. He must have struggled on for miles and any ordinary dog could never have survived. But somehow the stubborn cairn held on to his nefarious life long enough to pop out, bad-tempered and bedraggled, at a sewage farm. He smelt outrageously when he returned home and Butch forced him to sleep outdoors for a week.

The weather was warmer now and the gang spent long lazy hours in a nearby park. It was Scruffy's first summer and she'd never known the world so friendly before. It still snowed, but only pink and white blossom from the trees. The wind still blew, but caressingly and without malice, and even the rain felt good as she romped over the soft grass with Butch — nuzzling, teasing, eyeing each other with careless glances as coy young lovers do.

To Sam, however, a stroll in the park on a sunny day offered so much more. Here he could turn to thoughts of love — not that he ever thought of anything else, even in the depth of winter. But, at this time of year, the lady dogs seemed even more susceptible.

Hamlet would occasionally join them, provided it was out of opening hours, though his company usually meant more trouble than it was worth. Like the time he fell in the lake and would have surely drowned if Butch hadn't hauled him out by his ear. Solo's only activity in the park was gladiatorial. There was always something moving to get his teeth into.

Unlike Solo, Butch was not a dog that went looking for trouble. He would fight if he had to, and with indomitable courage. But his normal manner was genial and tolerant.

He did not want trouble the day the bull mastiff stalked Scruffy between the bushes, and even when the colossal animal blocked their path, bearing teeth like iron spikes, he still ignored it.

What he could not ignore, however, was when it lunged at Scruffy, bull-dozing the terrified bitch across the grass. Butch leapt to her side and stood facing the mastiff, the short hair along his back pricked in sudden and overwhelming fury, the muscles in his short statuesque body tensed for the battle that had to come.

The bull mastiff stared back, eyes slotted in hate, pendulous lips drawn — dwarfing its gutsy contender. Butch waited for it to make the first move. Even now he would have avoided bloodshed if the mastiff had withdrawn and gone on its way. He glanced at Scruffy who was trembling on the ground a few yards away and, in that split second of distraction, the monster pounced . . .

One hundred and thirty pounds of brawn and bone crunched into Butch's side with the kick of a mule, blasting the air from his lungs and tossing him onto his back. A second onslaught followed as the dazed terrier tried to regain his feet. This time the brute's front paws ground into his back like pile-drivers. Butch's misty eyes caught a glint of ivory in the sun. He tried to twist from the mastiff's smothering bulk but was too slow. The murderous teeth ripped across his shoulder and warm dark blood pumped through the glaring wound, streaking his fur as he rolled clear.

The mastiff crouched for the final attack. Butch stood up and lowered his head. Suddenly he was back in the fighting rings of his ferocious ancestors. He knew what had to be done. It was his life or the mastiff's. It was kill or be killed. There could be no half-measures now.

He crouched too, every muscle flexed, his slanting eyes fixed on the other's throat. When he made his move it was rapier-fast and savage. The mastiff could only half turn as Butch chose his spot and bit deep with vampire-like precision in the side of the neck. His fangs met through the folds of meaty skin and locked. Nothing would prise them open now.

The mastiff gave an agonised yelp and crashed to the ground. Butch straddled it, raking his claws across its back like spurs. Now he was a solid, compact fighting machine — indifferent to pain. The other dog lurched to its feet, thrashing its huge body from side to side like a harpooned whale, but those devilish jaws, dripping with the mastiff's blood, held on. It hurled itself through the air crashing backwards on top of Butch. The cracking rib had the thrust of a dagger and the terrier's head swam as he struggled to drag air between his throbbing jaws.

Wild with pain and terror, the mastiff clawed insanely along the ground with Butch slumped, barely conscious across its back. The challenge was over. Now all the distracted animal wanted was to escape the appalling torment. At last, in one hysterical lunge, it tore itself away, leaving the mangled flesh still between Butch's clenched fangs. The mastiff gave a soul-piercing cry and staggered off into the bushes.

With a supreme effort, Butch gathered his last vestige of strength to heave unsteadily to his feet. He stood there for a moment, eyes closed, head bowed, his exhausted body trembling and swaying about. Scruffy whimpered and scampered to his side as his legs crumpled beneath him. And there he lay, too weary to move a muscle, his steaming tongue twitching between lolling jaws, now numb from the terrible retribution they had just inflicted on a fighter more than twice his own weight.

Scruffy licked the cruel gash in his shoulder, huddling so close she could feel his tenacious heart battling to pump new life into the limp and useless frame. Then, very painfully, the crippled warrior hauled himself up and shuffled forward with short, wavering steps.

The journey home was mercilessly slow. Each time Butch stumbled to the pavement, Scruffy waited patiently for him to muster enough energy to try again. Halfway across the car lot he passed out. Scruffy dashed on ahead, barking furiously. The collie heard and leapt from the wrecked saloon, followed by Sam. When they saw their fallen champion they drew back, tipping their heads in disbelief. How could this happen to Butch? Butch was invincible.

Sam crouched a few feet away staring at the awful shoulder wound and whining like a werewolf. But the collie bustled around nudging the bull terrier's floppy limbs with her muzzle then sniffing his entire body, trying to assess the extent of the injuries. A cool, dust-laden gust of wind made the terrier shudder. The collie licked open one of his eye-lids then backed away, barking sternly as if telling him he must somehow get back to the car. He understood and heaved his shoulders a few inches from the ground, dragging himself along with his front legs. The collie lowered her own shoulder to the ground and thrust it against his rear, snapping at the mesmerised Sam to help her.

She got Butch as far as the car but knew she could not lift him inside. She considered for a moment then sprang onto the front seat. Scruffy was amazed when she returned with her piece of old blanket and draped it over Butch's back. No one had ever been permitted to use that before.

An hour later Solo arrived. He walked round the still figure, cursing softly. Served the bossy, overbearing bull terrier right. Something had obviously put him in his place, and about time too. He cuffed Butch's nose with his paw — something he'd wanted to do for a long time. A split second later he was flat on his back, pinned to the ground by two gigantic paws. Solo blinked in astonishment. They were Sam's. So were those lethal-looking fangs snarling at him only inches from his scraggy throat. The Alsatian must have gone completely off his head. Attacking him, Solo. It was ridiculous. The blundering idiot was even scared of cats. But, whatever it was that had suddenly come over Sam, he obviously meant business and the cairn decided it would be more prudent to deal with him later when he returned to his senses. When the Alsatian released him he sulked off to his seat in the car.

Hamlet weaved his way across the car lot and fell headlong over Butch's body. Scruffy's fur bristled and she yapped angrily at the drowsy boxer's clumsiness. He peered bleary-eyed at the bull terrier, quite unable to comprehend, then tottered backwards at the sight of caked blood across his leader's shoulder. He gave the collie a helpless look and started to howl.

Solo snarled at Hamlet's faint-heartedness. Battle injuries were not to be mourned. The cairn felt envy, not pity. He'd have been proud to sport a wound as magnificent as that.

Scruffy stayed at Butch's side, watching him intently throughout the long, cool night — jolting alert at every quiver of his streamlined frame, every flicker of his eyes or twitch of his bulging cheek muscles.

He seemed much better the next morning — more aware of things about him. But he was still very weak. He had lost a great deal of blood and his cracked rib stabbed painfully when he tugged himself into the back seat, where he collapsed, gasping huskily from the effort. Scruffy climbed alongside him, licking away the dark congealed blood from his coat. He looked at her, eyes heavy with devotion, and he sensed her pride in what he had done.

The collie woke the Alsatian with nagging yaps and he followed her across the car lot. Butch had to be fed and, apart from himself, Sam was the most accomplished scavenger. Scruffy was still tending Butch's shoulder when they returned a few hours later, each carrying huge bones, which they dropped onto the back seat. The bull terrier panted appreciatively and licked them. But it would be some time before those valiant jaws would have the strength to gnaw through bones again. However, the gesture reminded Scruffy that Butch would have to take nourishment soon if he was to recover. Old Hamlet must have realised this too. He arrived home much earlier than usual and dropped one of the Prince of Denmark's stodgy meat pies in his leader's lap.

The most remarkable thing happened next . . . something none of the dogs would have ever believed possible if they hadn't witnessed it with their own eyes. There was a clattering sound, like some metal object being dragged over the stony ground. When Butch discovered what it was he almost had a relapse. There, emerging backwards between the debris outside, was Solo, heaving along a tin dish with his teeth. It was half full of curried beef.

15

The days following his battle with the bull mastiff were critical ones for Butch. A weak leader was vulnerable. As in all groups of animals — whether they be rabbits or rhinoceroses — nature decrees that only the stronget shall rule. It has to be so if the pack as a whole is to survive. Butch realised that unless he consolidated his dominance quickly, he could lose it forever.

Fortunately, there was no obvious male successor among the group. Sam, the largest and most imposing animal, was far too submissive. Hamlet, of course, was in no condition to even head a flock of sheep. Solo was the only member with the courage to depose Butch and, if he had been bigger, doubtlessly would have done so.

Oddly enough, the little cairn now seemed as determined as any of them to retain the bull terrier's leadership. For one thing he was somewhat perturbed by Sam's sudden show of strength. Not that the Alsatian had tried anything on since. But it confused him. Another thing was that, despite the cairn's outward defiance, he knew, deep down inside, that Butch was really the best of the bunch. In fact it was probably Solo's regular diet of curried beef that put Butch back on his feet after less than a week.

Apart from her sorties for food, which usually took

in a hasty visit to the shrine of Joseph Tibbles, Scruffy had remained at Butch's side night and day. The torn shoulder healed nicely though the cracked rib was still painful and she knew he would have to take things easy for a while. However, the bull terrier was eager to re-establish himself.

The morning he headed into town Scruffy padded diligently along too. Their first call was the newspaper-seller's pitch. He greeted Butch like a long-lost son. The dog winced as he patted the injured shoulder and the man whipped his hand away.

'Crikey, fella,' he gasped, 'that's nasty. What the devil's been happening to you?' He glanced at Scruffy. 'Don't tell me she did it.' The bitch licked the shoulder as he spoke. 'No, I can see she didn't. Seems to think a lot of you, doesn't she Butch?' He delved into his pocket and handed out generous helpings of biscuits. 'There,' he smiled warmly, 'I'll put you both on double rations this week.' He rubbed his chin. 'It wasn't that villainous Solo, was it? No, I don't think so. He'd be dead by now — and I've seen him once or twice recently dragging a tin dish about with him. An odd thing to do now I come to think of it.' He grinned. 'Anyway, whoever it was, heaven help them, that's all I can say. I'll bet they took a right old thrashing.'

The dogs finished the biscuits and carried on their way. There were few pickings that morning. Chop suey was out of the question. Butch knew he dare not risk a restaurant raid. If he was spotted he would have been in no condition to make a run for it. By late afternoon they were both very hungry.

As a last resort Butch led his companion across town to the docks. He'd been there before. He knew that if a food ship had been unloaded that day there would be a fair chance of finding edible left-overs. But there was nothing. The area had been swept clean and the only cargo being swung ashore was industrial machinery.

They were about to leave when Butch noticed an enormous Old English sheepdog. It was sitting on the quayside, still as a haystack, gazing across the murky water and twitching its big black nose in the breeze. What particularly interested the bull terrier, however, was the dish at its side, piled high with meat. He moved nearer and watched for a while from behind a wooden crate. It seemed totally disinterested in the food. Knowing most old English sheepdogs to be of a placid, open-hearted disposition, Butch dropped onto his belly and approached to within a few feet, waving his tail like a flag of truce.

The doleful dog still ignored him and continued to stare blankly up the river. The bull-terrier inched forward, grabbed a mouthful of meat and sprang back. Nothing happened so he stretched his neck over the dish and carried on eating, keeping a cautious eye on the sheepdog in case it suddenly withdrew its astonishing hospitality. But he might not have been there for all the other cared.

Butch saved the largest chunks of meat to take back to Scruffy. As she ate, three burly dockers ambled towards the sheepdog. It still didn't respond when one of them patted its head. 'Ah, you've eaten it this time, have you?' he smiled affectionately. 'That's a good lad.' He turned to his colleagues. 'Reckon he's getting over it a bit.'

'Could be. It's the first meal he's eaten for three days.'

'Getting over what?' asked the third man.

'Old Gerry Taylor, skipper of the Magpie.'

'What, you mean that pleasure boat that chugs up and down the river?'

'That's right.'

'Didn't the poor bloke have a heart attack or something a month or two ago?'

'Yes. Dropped dead in the wheel-house. They took him ashore a few miles back.'

'And this is his dog?'

'That's it. They thought the world of each other. It's waited here for the Magpie to come in every day since it was a pup. Knows the docking times better than the crew.'

'But what's it doing here now?'

The first man ran his beefy fingers through the dog's fur. 'Still waiting. Doesn't realise the skipper's dead, I suppose. It still meets the boat. Never misses a trip.'

'What, every day?'

'Yes, it waits for hours. That's why we bring its food here.' The man hooked his hand through the dog's collar. 'Come on lad — time to go home now. There're no more sailings today.' The dog followed him, whimpering softly. It would be back, of course, even though it stood as much chance of seeing old Gerry Taylor steaming in on the Magpie as Scruffy had of finding Joseph P. Tibbles snoozing underneath the arches.

Butch was feeling very tired now and his wounds were causing considerable pain. He had obviously done too much. On their way home they passed Solo. Butch gave a friendly bark but the cairn carried on, cussing to himself. He knew it wouldn't be long before that pompous bull terrier was ordering him about again. But when Butch reached the car he gave Scruffy a knowing glance. There was a full dish of curried beef waiting for him inside. And, squelched on the back seat, was another of Hamlet's sloppy meat pies. What clearer votes of confidence could any leader ask?

August was a bad time for Solo. His friend at the Indian restaurant went off to visit a cousin in Bombay and the supply of curried beef dried up for three weeks. The rest of the gang would have no doubt been quite willing to share their food with him but *he* wasn't going to admit his dependence on anyone. He'd manage somehow. However, it wasn't easy. He'd made too many enemies around town. The only hand-outs he got were clips across the ears, and he was too small to raid dustbins.

After a few days he was getting desperate. He had to find some temporary source of food to tide him over. He considered the problem. Accepting charity from Butch or the Alsatian was out of the question, and he certainly wasn't prepared to go dish-in-paw to the bitches. That only left Hamlet. Yes — *he* might be the answer. Hamlet and his meat pies. He'd find out where the fuddled old thing got them.

That evening he trailed Hamlet to the Prince of Denmark. When the boxer went inside he waited on the step spying through a gap in the door. Hamlet stopped at one of the tables. Then he sat up on his flabby haunches, lost his balance and sprawled over backwards. Everyone roared and one of the customers snapped his fingers at the barmaid. 'Two pints love,' he cried, 'and the usual for the dog.'

Solo watched the man tilt a glass for Hamlet to lap its frothy contents. An hour later people were still ordering re-fills for the insatiable boxer. The cairn was about to turn away in digust when a man at the counter strolled over and dropped a half-eaten pie at Hamlet's feet. Solo's mouth watered. Another customer did the same. The cairn wagged his tail. There was nothing to it. All he had to do was sit up, fall down, drink whatever he was offered and wait for the meat pies.

There was only one snag. He couldn't do it here. He couldn't demean himself by begging in front of a member of his own gang. He'd have to perform somewhere else.

Solo hurried off along the street to the next place with the same smell. The door was ajar and he poked his nose through. Yes, it looked very similar to Hamlet's haunt. He wriggle inside and marched boldly to the nearest table, sat up, fell down and rolled over on his back. It worked. Everyone roared, and a man seated at the table nudged his companion. 'I think it's asking for a drink, Fred. Let's buy it one — just for a laugh.'

He patted the cairn's back — a gesture that normally might have cost him part of a finger if Solo hadn't needed to butter him up — and walked to the counter. 'Got a spare pint pot love,' he asked the barmaid, 'I think the little chap's thirsty.' She half-filled a glass from one of the pumps. 'Here nipper,' chuckled the man holding it in front of the cairn.

The dog sniffed and heaved. Was it worth it? But he eyed a stack of pies on the counter and decided it was. However, the only way he could reach the liquid with his short tongue was to stuff the whole of his head inside the glass. This he accomplished. Unfortunately once inside, it jammed tight. No doubt the man could have eased it off if the cairn had remained calm. But Solo couldn't breathe and he panicked.

With a muffled howl that seemed to come from a long way off, he skidded madly about the room and, as another customer entered the door, Solo darted between his legs and pounded blindly along the pavement. An instant later there was a sickening crash of exploding glass as the cairn battered head first into the nearest lamp-post, knocking himself senseless.

It was some time before Solo could see straight enough to head for home and anyone watching him weave along the street would have sworn he'd drunk more than Hamlet.

The newspaper-seller was surprised the morning he saw the entire gang on the move (with the exception of Solo, of course). He knew they normally hunted singly or in pairs. They were in a desperate hurry too. Butch was galloping along at the front and flashed by without even a glance at his kindly old benefactor. Scruffy and Sam were hard on the bull terrier's heels and the collie — her Wellington boot flopping between her jaws — followed, with Hamlet wheezing along some distance behind.

The reason for the stampede became obvious as Mr. Wang from the Chinese restaurant came hurtling round a corner wielding his meat cleaver like an Apache warrior. Hamlet looked back and swung off along a narrow alley, where he crouched exhausted as the man puffed on after the others. But they were well out of range and he leaned against a wall, shaking his cleaver at them and muttering the most devilish-sounding incantations.

Butch still drove his companions on and, with the traffic signals in their favour, they all hared across the next junction. On reaching the opposite pavement the collie swung round. She had dropped her boot in the middle of the road. Before the others could stop her she leapt from the kerb and tore back to retrieve it. The moment she did so, the traffic lights changed. Butch barked a frantic warning but he knew she couldn't hear him . . . any more than she could hear the lorry suddenly thunder round the bend. There was a snarling of brakes as the collie snapped up the boot and started back across the road. Scruffy closed her eyes in horror. The dull crunch that followed tossed the collie high into the air. She thudded onto the lorry's metal bonnet and rolled off into the gutter, where she lay motionless.

The lorry stopped and the ashen-faced driver jumped from his cab and cradled the limp collie in his arms. A woman shopper, trembling and wringing her hands, shouted: 'I'll fetch the vet. His surgery's only in the next street. Try not to move the poor thing.'

The news-seller, who had seen everything, hurried over and knelt by the lorry-driver's side, 'Looks bad,' he murmured. 'Don't think a vet'll be much use now.' The other shook his head. 'There was nothing I could do,' he said in a croaky voice. 'It suddenly flew back into the road for that.' He lifted the heel of the rubber boot. 'Why? It doesn't make sense. I mean if it'd been a bone or something I could understand. It didn't have a chance, poor little devil.'

The older man rubbed the side of his nose. 'No, it is odd. I've wondered about that boot. Never seen the animal without it. Seems to have taken its fancy. Dogs are funny creatures sometimes.'

When the vet carried the collie to his surgery the lorry-driver went too. The former nodded when he heard what the dog had done. 'Ah, yes,' he explained, 'it's what's known as a phantom pregnancy.' He began to examine the lifeless animal. 'It's not all that uncommon. You see, this is a bitch. It's my guess she hasn't been able to have pups for some reason. But the maternal instinct's still there. She's probably been going through all the usual symptoms associated with a real pregnancy — even to producing milk. It's something to do with hormone balance. I've known bitches become attached to all kinds of things . . . chicks, kittens, even a child's teddy bear. They'll nurse and defend them just as they would pups of their own. This one must have adopted a Wellington boot.' The other man turned away as the back of his hand left damp streaks across his cheek. 'But she'll be all right,' added the vet chirpily. 'Look, she's coming round nicely. Just stunned, that's all.' The lorry-driver beamed and grabbed his wrist. 'You sure?' The vet nodded as the collie looked up with round, sorrowful eyes. 'Suppose I'd better inform the police.'

'Must you?'

'Well there's no collar. She's obviously a stray and I can't keep her here.'

The driver bit his lip. 'You won't have to. Give her to me. I'll take her home, it's the least I can do. And anyway the wife'll love her.'

The collie was now sitting up and looking quite perky. The man clapped his hands. 'There, that's better. Coming with me, are you?' The vet half-smiled. 'It's no use — she can't hear you, you know.'

'How d'you mean?'

'I've been watching her reactions — or rather, lack of them. She's stone deaf.'

The other tried to swallow the lump in his throat and put an arm over the dog's shoulder. 'So — who cares? We'll sort something out, won't we old girl?'

He carried the collie very carefully out of the surgery to his lorry and placed her in the passenger seat. The rest of the gang were still lined up on the far side of the road. The man was about to switch on his engine when Butch gave a loud, hollow bark. As the driver glanced at the bull terrier, he noticed the Wellington boot lying in the gutter. He climbed out of the cab, picked it up and placed it in the collie's lap. 'Crikey,' he said warmly, 'I nearly forgot. Can't go home without junior, can we?'

16

Butch had led the gang for three years. It wasn't that he disliked humans; on the contrary. But for his overpowering devotion for them he might still have been enjoying regular meals and the luxury of his own basket by someone's fireside.

He had started life with a pair of newly-weds. As a pup they had encouraged his boisterous affection. Whenever the man returned from work he would hold out his arms and Butch (or whatever name he answered to in those days) would leap into them, licking his master's face all over. But the bull terrier was a sturdily built one-year-old when the new baby arrived, and twice his joyful exuberance had toppled it out of its plastic carry-cot. Not only that, but the district nurse had a fervent distrust of all domestic pets and had convinced the infant's mother that they were the carriers of just about everything from nappy-rash to the black plague. The man had defended his lovable young companion with arguments that raged late into the night. But, as always in such matters, new mothers invariably get their way in the end. 'It's the dog or me,' was the final straw she had uttered with a flourish, and that was that. The dog had to go.

There were lots of tears, of course, when the bewildered bull terrier was handed over to an elderly woman answering their 'Good Home Wanted' advertisement in the evening newspaper. But Butch was soon happy to lavish his unrestrained loyalty on his new owner. Unfortunately, after he'd knocked her down numerous times and finally broken her wrist in three places, the little woman's patronage waned. She took Butch for the longest walk of his life, tied him to a tree and caught the first bus home alone.

Some children had released him the next day. He had wandered into town and eventually taken up residence in the wrecked car lot. Hamlet had moved in a few weeks later. Then came the collie, Solo and Sam.

Butch was looking at them all now, lounging by the car in the weak September sunlight, and he suddenly felt it was time to move on. He was proud to have been their leader for so long and none of them were disputing his authority even now. But, though the injuries inflicted by the bull mastiff were healed, he knew he was no longer the dog he used to be. He knew he had neither the stamina nor the will to accept responsibility for them all much longer, or to put on continually the show of strength they had every right to expect of him.

He instinctively realised, too, that soon some younger, fitter dog would certainly challenge him and take over, and nothing could be more humiliating than that. Once a leader is deposed he must accept the most menial rank in the pack. And anyway, let's face it, they were a rum lot to be in charge of. Wet nursing Hamlet was beginning to get him down; Solo was becoming more belligerent than ever, launching himself at the biggest animals he could find like a tiny kamikaze pilot; and big Sam was even more dependent on him since the collie left. All in all, he'd had enough. It was time to take things easier.

He felt Scruffy twitch in her sleep and turned to lick her ear. Life would be so much simpler for just the two of them. They could find a place of their own. Perhaps even have a family. Yes, that was it. He'd start looking around.

The following day Butch and Scruffy trotted off together as usual. It was after they'd collected the news-seller's biscuits and raided a Chinese restaurant that Butch started weighing up possible new lodgings. Naturally enough he thought of these in terms of motor cars. There were plenty around, but most were already tenanted by humans.

Butch found some temporarily unoccupied ones parked on a slope outside a row of shops. They were beauties — glossy and well upholstered, with draught-free windows and all mod cons. He knew such extravagance was not for the likes of Scruffy and him, but there seemed no harm in just looking. He glanced around. The only humans were busy inside the shops, so he stretched his front legs against one of the cars and peered through the open window. It was sheer luxury and his nostrils throbbed to the rich, tangy smell of real leather. What a home this would make!

As his paws slid down the shiny metal door, one of them caught a chromium-plated handle. It clicked and the door swung ajar. The temptation was too much to ignore. Butch crept inside and Scruffy followed. It was like a palace and they sniffed in every corner. As they did so, Butch's broad back bumped against a lever jutting below the steering wheel, nudging the gear selector into neutral. This would not have mattered if the careless motorist hadn't left the handbrake off.

Neither dog noticed the car was moving downhill until the front wheels mounted the kerb with a jolt. Butch scrambled onto the seat. There was a deafening crash and shattered glass peppered the roof like gunshot. When the bull terrier stared out, the shiny radiator of the car was where a large plate-glass window had been.

Pandemonium followed as the dogs sprang from the car and scorched off along the pavement. Half a dozen people tried to hurl themselves through the shop door at the same time, as a woman at the back swooned against the counter. 'It's ours George, it's ours!' she screamed hysterically. The man next to her elbowed his way out as someone shouted: 'It was those scatty dogs — didn't you see them?' The man wailed: 'Oh no . . . the insurance people'll never believe this.' The shopkeeper grabbed his arm and dragged him along the pavement. 'Come on then, let's get 'em, and quick!' The other yelled over his shoulder: 'Ring the police, Elsie . . .' and dashed off after the shopkeeper.

Three or four others joined the chase as the dogs skidded round the block and ducked along the first alley they came to. Scruffy glanced back. The enraged pursuers were storming up the alley waving their arms and urging anyone else within ear-shot to 'Stop those dogs?' A man passing the alley exit tried, but Butch skirted round him and the bitch darted between his legs. To an anguished fanfare of motor horns, the dogs plunged across the busy street. Women shoppers threw up their hands and squealed as Scruffy streaked between the front and rear wheels of a moving lorry. Then everything stopped as the angry shopkeeper and his posse dodged through the traffic like a pack of foxhounds.

The dogs pelted on and bobbed into a narrow entry between the shops. Other cobbled passages led off it. They swerved into one of these and slid to a halt. It was a dead end! Butch doubled back then stopped. He could hear the mob pounding towards them. They both pressed their bodies against a wall as the stampede thundered passed.

The dogs stayed where they were until the clattering footsteps died away. Scruffy was exhausted and Butch was getting niggling stabs of pain from the rib he had cracked eight weeks before. They were about to creep out of the cul-de-sac when they heard more footsteps — slower, heavier ones. Butch found himself staring at two pairs of great black boots as a voice above boomed: 'Here they are sergeant!'

Butch barked to Scruffy, slithered between the two policemen and belted off along the entry. But the bitch stayed pinned to the wall in terror. She couldn't move. The bull terrier turned. Scruffy was tucked under the sergeant's arm like an old hearthrug and was looking at him with pleading eyes. 'Let's get this one in the car,' said the officer, 'The other won't get far.'

Butch's first instinct was to escape into the maze of streets he knew so well. He started to run, then hesitated, spun round and hurried back along the entry. When he reached the end a blue police car was pulling away from the kerb. Scruffy was peering through the rear window. Butch was suddenly convinced that freedom without her meant nothing any more and, blind to everything else, he tore after the car. The policeman at the wheel spotted him in his driving mirror. 'There's the other one,' he gaped, 'The barmy animal's actually chasing us.' His companion twisted in his seat. 'That's odd. Pull over.'

The car stopped and the sergeant climbed out. To his astonishment Butch flew straight past him and leapt onto the back seat next to Scruffy. The car moved off again and the pair of them snuggled up together. The sergeant watched and shook his head. 'Well now,' he muttered warmly, 'that's true love if ever I saw it. Just look at 'em — billing and cooing like a couple of turtle doves.'

Ten minutes later the dogs were lying in a stone-flagged yard, roped to a large wooden kennel. There were angry voices as two men burst through the rear door of the police station. 'That's them all right,' cried one, 'I'll strangle that bull terrier!' The sergeant held the shopkeeper back as he flung himself towards Butch. 'Steady on, sir,' he said, '. . . no need for that.' The other tried to prise his arm from the officer's steely grip, but failed. 'Have you seen my shop front?' he bellowed. 'It's a shambles. Go and look.'

His crimson-faced companion joined in. 'And what about my car? I've only had it a week. What am I going to tell the insurance people?' Scruffy cowered against the kennel as the officer ushered the men into the station. 'Now calm down both of you,' he said firmly. 'We'll sort everything out in the charge office.'

It was some time before a uniformed clerk had laboriously entered details of the accident in a thick leather-bound book. As the shopkeeper and the car owner stormed off, an important-looking man with a bow-tie moustache strode into the office. 'Those dogs . . .' he snapped. '. . . is one of them a mangy Alsatian?' The sergeant stiffened. 'Afraid not inspector.'

'Blast,' barked the other. 'I'm sick to death of

getting complaints about that one.' As he stalked away a policeman thrust his head round the yard door. 'Excuse me, sir,' he called sheepishly. The inspector swung round. 'What is it Sixty-three?'

'You were asking about the Alsatian.'

'Well?'

'It used to be in the force sir.'

'It *what!*'

The policeman winced. 'Er . . . it was a police dog with D. Division some years ago.'

The inspector groaned and closed his eyes. 'Oh no, that's all I need to know. For pity's sake, Sixty-three, keep it to yourself. If those complaining residents find out the villain was one of ours we'll look real Charlies.'

'Yes sir.'

'What!'

'I mean no, sir . . . er I won't say a word, sir.'

The inspector's eyes narrowed and swept round the charge office. 'Now listen to me, all of you,' he snarled. 'I want that cursed animal, so think of something . . . and fast. Understand?' Everyone nodded furiously.

When he'd gone they stood round eyeing each other in glum silence. Then one of them said. 'We know where to find the Alsatian, sergeant. He's always prowling around that housing estate near the docks. He's after the bitches. It's their owners who have made most of the complaints. But we've never been able to get near him. Reckon he'd be a rough handful if he turned nasty.' P.C. Sixty-three shook his head. 'Oh, he's not vicious. That's why D. Division got rid of him. Wouldn't harm a fly.'

The sergeant said nothing for a while, then he thwacked his palm on the table. 'I think I've got it,' he cried. They all gathered round. 'Now listen. He's a lady-killer . . . right?' The others nodded. 'So, we'll play him at his own game. We'll bait him with one of our bitches. It's been done before. We'll put her in a van and park it near the estate.' They all marvelled at his ingenuity and P.C. Sixty-three put the kettle on.

Later as they supped from steaming mugs of tea, someone asked: 'Shall I tell the dogs' home about the two out there?' The sergeant shook his head. 'No, not yet. That pesky motorist might want to bring his insurance man round to see them. We'll keep them here for a few days.'

One of the policemen strolled into the yard. Butch was asleep with Scruffy's head on his shoulder. 'Poor little blighters,' he mumbled, patting the bull terrier's head. 'I'd turn you both loose mate . . . but it's more than my job's worth.'

17

That night, back at the wrecked car lot, only Hamlet slept, and this was simply because he was too tipsy to realise his leader was missing.

Big Sam stayed wide awake until dawn gazing at Butch's empty place on the rear seat and Solo paced up and down outside cursing to himself non-stop. The cairn was convinced Butch had deserted . . . besotted by that goo-goo-eyed little bitch he'd brought home. He'd always known she'd be trouble one day. The love-sick bull terrier wasn't fit to rule the roost after this and he, Solo, would make that very clear when he came strutting back expecting everyone to start taking orders again. He snarled. And to think that not long ago he had squandered mountains of curried beef to save his miserable life.

However, Solo spent the whole of the following day frantically searching each of Butch's known haunts, becoming more dispirited all the time. When the crisis eventually seeped into Hamlet's befuddled brain, he too scoured the town alongside the demoralized Sam until their paws were raw and the unhappy boxer was too fatigued to even pay his nightly respects to the Prince of Denmark.

It was three days after Butch and Scruffy had been taken into custody that the police van passed Sam and Hamlet on the housing estate near the docks. 'That's the one the inspector wants,' the driver shouted. 'I'll park round the corner.'

'D'you think he'll fall for it?' asked his colleague.

The driver looked over his shoulder at a sleek, immaculately-groomed Alsatian chained in the back of the van. 'If his reputation's anything to go by he won't be able to resist this one. She's a beauty.'

'Seems a bit sneaky nabbing the old trouper this way.' The other nodded. 'Yes, I suppose it is. But it's got to be done. The boss has been on the warpath all week.' He turned into a side road and stopped. 'Open the back doors and keep out of sight behind that garden hedge.'

Sam's Olympean flame of passion was kindled from fully fifty yards. Instantly bewitched by the rapturous scent of the bitch, he bounded from Hamlet's side straight into the van. The boxer yapped a warning as the policeman popped round the hedge. But it was too late. The van doors slammed shut.

Hamlet sat on the kerb and watched the vehicle move off, the downcast face of his dear friend flattened against the rear window looking back at him with reproachful eyes. Sam had met his Delilah.

Butch's tail beat the flagstone when the Alsatian was led into the police station yard. There was a warm reunion with welcoming sniffs all round and, despite his capitivity, Sam felt safe and happy again. He was back with his beloved leader and that was all he cared about.

That evening the owner of the car Butch had crashed through the shop window called with his insurance man. As they left, the sergeant beckoned P.C. Sixty-three. 'Well,' he sighed, 'that's that. They'll pay for the repairs to his precious motor car. And copping that Alsatian's put the inspector in a better mood. I'm off.' He turned back at the door. 'Oh yes — you can ring the dogs' home now. Tell them we've got three new clients. You can take them round in the morning.'

No dog could ever have felt lonelier than Hamlet as he'd watched Sam being taken away in the police van. Now he had no one to whom he could turn and he certainly didn't fancy spending the rest of his days with that cantankerous little cairn.

He wandered the streets until opening time, then waddled his way to the Prince of Denmark. The landlord could tell something was bothering him. He only managed to get down half a pint and wouldn't even touch a meat pie. 'D'you think he's sickening for something?' suggested the barmaid. 'It's not like him, is it?'

'Suppose he must be. But all dogs have their ups and downs. He'll probably be all right by tomorrow. They sleep these things off usually.'

The barmaid wasn't really convinced. 'Oh I do hope you're right. I've sort of got used to the funny old thing. I'd hate to think he was suffering.'

'Don't worry. Tell you what — if he's no better in a couple of days I'll get a vet to have a look at him.'

Hamlet couldn't bring himself to return to the car lot that night so he slept on the hotel step. The next morning he ambled to the park where he curled up on the grass, watching people walking their pets round the lake. He could vaguely recall someone doing that with him a long time ago. He was a handsome, well-groomed animal in those days, and the pride of the elderly vicar who owned him. He was quite valuable too, which was the reason he'd been dog-napped by a couple of unsavoury characters in a stolen van. They had driven him miles from his home village but he'd escaped before they'd had a chance to sell him and he had been on the run ever since.

Now he suddenly felt a deep yearning to belong to someone again. He was tired of living rough. Tired of begging. He was too long in the molars to think of joining another gang even if one would have him, and he couldn't face a long cruel winter alone. No, the time had come to return to the safe, predictable world of Man, and there and then he decided he would ingratiate himself on the first likely human to cross his path.

The victim turned out to be a small, middle-aged schoolteacher who was unwary enough to pat Hamlet's head. It was all the boxer needed and he adopted her forthwith. The poor woman was soon to regret having set foot in the park that blustery day.

He followed her along the edge of the lake and, when she perched on a bench, Hamlet did his one and only party trick — sitting up and falling over onto his back. The woman whinnied in delight and bent down to rub his podgy stomach. Unfortunately, she smelt his breath at the same time and swooned. That did it. She jumped to her feet and walked off with her nose in the air. Hamlet padded after her. He was all her's now. He couldn't wait to get his head down on her hearthrug.

The woman glanced back, quickening her pace. So did Hamlet. She swung round stamping her tiny brogue-shod foot. 'Shoo, shoo,' she snapped, '. . . go home now, there's a good boy.' But Hamlet was most persistent — *dog*matic you might say. He stayed right there at her heels as she swept out of the park and hastened along the pavement. She dodged into a bookshop and hid behind the shelves, but Hamlet waited patiently outside. He was determined not to lose her.

He was still dogging her when she burst through the front door of her neat detached house and locked it in Hamlet's face. But, after trailing her this far, the boxer had no intention of giving her up now. With a wheezy sigh he flopped on the step. And there he stayed, watching the woman having palpitations each time she peeked through her lace curtains.

He was still there at dusk as the distracted woman talked to her friend on the telephone for the third time. 'Yes Gertrude,' she was saying, '. . . outside on the step . . . Oh no, it isn't vicious or anything like that — quite a friendly old thing, but ooh Gertrude, you should smell its breath. It's like a brewery . . . Yes, perhaps you're right. Perhaps it'll go home when it's hungry . . . thanks dear, you're very kind, but I think I'll be all right . . . I'll give you a ring in the morning. Bye Gertrude.'

'Hello Gertrude. It's Mabel. This is terrible — it's still out there. Hasn't budged all night . . . What's that? You're coming round? Ooh, do be careful, it's turned funny . . . Well it's stopping anyone getting passed the front gate. It's already gone for the postman and the newspaper boy and it won't let me out of the house. It must think it's guarding me. It's all very alarming. I just don't know what to do . . . What's that Gertrude? The police? D'you think I should? Yes, all right — I'll ring you back.'

Police Constable Sixty-three groaned when he picked up the telephone in the charge office. 'Oh no

— not another blooming dog,' he muttered to himself. He handed the receiver to the sergeant. 'She wants to speak to you.'

The other screwed up his face as he listened. '. . . You say it's been there all night? . . . What's that? . . . Trapped, madam? Trapped in your own home? . . . Won't let anyone in or out? . . . Just a minute.' He jabbed his finger at the door. 'Get round to twenty-two Acacia Avenue fast. The flaming animal's holding half the neighbourhood at bay.'

P.C. Sixty-three hurried out. 'Yes madam . . .' drawled the sergeant, '. . . I'm still here. Yes, I understand . . . don't panic now, our chap's on his way. He'll be round there in five minutes. Just don't do anything . . . You what? It's after the man from the Prudential? . . . Yes, well I'm sure we'll sort it out . . . five minutes, yes.'

Hamlet had the white-faced insurance man pinned to the front gate when the police van drew up. P.C. Sixty-three leaned across waving his arms in front of the dog's face. 'Down boy,' he roared, '. . . down I say.' The boxer slid from the man's trembling legs and loped back to the front step, snarling in a most uncharacteristic manner. The officer hesitated and swallowed hard. He'd never admitted it to anyone, but he was petrified of dogs. It was a relief, therefore, when a man stopped his car and stretched over the privet hedge shouting: 'Hang on officer — I know how to handle him.'

'Thank goodness for that,' mumbled the policeman under his breath, as the man ducked into his car and returned with a bottle of stout. 'Ask the woman in the house to hand me a dish,' he said.

He poured the stout into it. 'Here Hamlet,' he coaxed, 'here fella, come and get it. It's my round.'

The policeman watched in astonishment as the boxer lapped up every drop. 'Cheers,' grinned the man pouring out the rest. As Hamlet drank this the officer deftly slipped a choke lead round his neck. 'Thanks sir,' he beamed, touching his helmet. 'I could have managed of course, but thanks all the same.'

'That's all right,' said the other. 'I thought it'd do the trick. He's a regular at the Prince of Denmark like me. Can't understand him carrying on like he did. He's normally such a good-natured soul.'

Hamlet made no more fuss. There seemed no point. In any case he was beginning to get the impression he'd overstayed his welcome. The fickle-minded woman could find herself another guard dog. He allowed the policeman to bustle him into the van.

When the officer tied him to the kennel in the station yard he sniffed all round it wagging his short tail. They'd been here. Butch and Sam and Scruffy. Their scent was unmistakable. He lay down contentedly. When they came back things would be just like they used to be.

In the charge office the weary sergeant pushed the telephone across to P.C. Sixty-three. 'Here,' he ordered, 'ring the dogs' home and tell 'em we've got another one.'

Meanwhile, at that very moment a mile away, a demented veterinary surgeon was doing his best to subdue a savage little cairn that seemed intent on amputating his fingers. It was Solo. An hour before, someone had brought him in unconscious. He'd had a most shocking experience. He'd cocked his leg against a metal 'keep left' bollard. There had been a blinding flash. Then a bang. And he'd been hurled halfway across the road onto his back — knocked out cold.

It appears the wet bollard was 'live' and the instant Solo did what he had to do, the jet completed the lectrical circuit. Now he had regained consciousness and was fighting mad as usual. The vet finally nanaged to tie a bandage round his snapping jaws and was ringing the police station . . .

Number Sixty-three couldn't speak for a few seconds when he answered the call. 'Sergeant,' he wailed softly '. . . you're never going to believe this.' The other's face sagged in despair. 'Don't tell me . . . another crazy dog?'

'Yes — the vet's bringing it in now. Seems it's blown up a traffic bollard.'

'It's what! Look Sixty-three, I'm in no mood for larking about.'

'Honest, sergeant.'

'Now listen to me. We've already had a dog that drives cars; we've had a sex-mad Alsatian; and we've had a house under siege by a drunken boxer. But this, Sixty-three . . . this is ridiculous! How the devil can a dog blow up a bollard?' He thumped the desk as the other was about to explain. 'No, no — *don't* tell me. I don't want to know. Just ring the dogs' home again and try to convince them we're not all stark raving mad. And when the perishing thing gets here, pack it off with that cross-eyed goon in the yard. I've had enough.'

18

Death Row at the home for strays was like a canine Alcatraz — especially in the moonlight when the long thin shadows of iron bars made convicts of the sleeping inmates.

It was a place where every dog had its day . . . printed in bold letters on metal plaques affixed to each cell like tombstones. There were Monday dogs, Tuesday Dogs and Wednesday dogs. Dogs, in fact, for every day of the week except Sunday.

It was a simple enough system. If a stray was brought in on Monday it was put in a Monday cell. If no one bailed it out by the following Monday, it took its last walk to the execution chamber at the end of the yard.

Daily intakes came from all parts of town. They were, in the main, an unprepossessing lot . . . collarless, flea-ridden and mangy with kicked-around looks, ribs like xylophones and eyes full of back-alley fear and suspicion. Few were reprieved — perhaps three in ten. For a dog to end up here usually meant somebody was glad to be rid of it. Maybe it was eating too much, chasing too many cats or simply getting under too many feet.

Scruffy, Butch and Sam arrived on Tuesday morning. They were, therefore, placed in a Tuesday cell. It was long and narrow with ten-foot bars. The

Alsatian was terrified and barged backwards and forwards, sniffing the cold concrete floor. Twice he tripped over a ragged little Yorkshire terrier that was lying on its stomach, limp in disillusion. Like themselves, it was in custody for having no visible means of support — particularly appropriate as you couldn't see its legs for long matted hair.

In complete contrast, a lofty, well-groomed bloodhound eyed the new arrivals with the severity of a high court judge, its wig-like ears cascading over great jowls that drooped in disapproval. This majestic animal was one of the few 'short-termers'. Someone was bound to claim him. And he knew it. There was nothing cowering or submissive about him. He was lolling against a wall with monumental self-assurance, smugly aware that his owner would be having pink fits wondering where he'd got to. But for most of the others, the dogs' home was the end of the road. And they seemed to know it.

Butch looked out at the other cell blocks situated on all sides of the open yard. He'd never seen so many dogs at one time or listened to such a bedlam of barks. It was a tormented ear-shattering symphony of yapping terriers, croupy old collies, yodelling spaniels and various other hounds of every size and shape imaginable.

Two men in overalls strolled around peering into the cells and Butch pricked his ears when they stopped to talk. 'This is today's little lot,' said one. He was short and plump with kind eyes. 'Pitiful, isn't it? I've been doing this job for years but I don't suppose I'll ever get used to the looks on their faces. No wonder they call this place Heartbreak House.'

His companion, whose sleeves and trouser legs were uncomfortably short for his long skinny limbs, was clearly new to the work. 'D'you reckon anyone'll take them, George?' he asked half-heartedly.

'Doubt it, Arthur.' The first man poked a finger into the Tuesday cell. 'Take Moses over there — he's not very elegant is he?'

'Moses?'

'The Yorkshire terrier.'

'Why is he called that, George?'

'I give 'em all names while they're with us. Some kids discovered this one tied up in a sack. It was half-submerged in the reeds of a river bank just down the road. That's how baby Moses was found, wasn't he? At least it's what they used to tell us at Sunday school.'

'Ah, I see. Yes — very apt.'

The other drew him to the next cell. 'Now these three pups were brought in together. I've nicknamed them Faith, Hope and Charity. They're going to need it too. It's their last day tomorrow.'

The new kennelman shook his head. 'Is the place always as crowded as this? There must be a couple of hundred of them.'

'Mostly. It's scandalous really. That terrier with the wonky legs, for instance, was found tied to a tree. It'd dug itself a hole in the ground . . . a sort of nest. Look at it — it's obvious no one fed it for days. We've even had unwanted pets left outside the gates at night. Not just young ones. Some have been old and blind. They've obviously been house-dogs for years. How can anyone dump a dog like that? It beats me, it really does.'

He glanced back at Faith, Hope and Charity, entwined together in sleep. 'Sometimes a bitch will actually have a litter of puppies while she's here and they've all to be put down with her. It's such a shame

— just being born to die like that. But there's no way we could keep them longer than we do.'

'D'you think dogs *know* when their time's up, George?'

''Course they do. They're far more sensitive than you think. The fox terrier over there, for example. Have you ever seen a more woeful expression than that? He knows all right.'

'Do they make a fuss?'

'Some do. We have to carry one or two of them. They won't take the last walk. But most seem to go quietly enough. We've very gentle, of course. We make a fuss and pacify them as best we can.' He looked up into his colleague's face. It was almost as downcast as the fox terrier's. 'You sure you want this job?' he asked softly. The other shrugged. 'I'll try to get used to it.'

People say animals can't talk. But they can. Not with their voices — with their eyes. In Butch's there was searing humiliation and, despite his passive silence, he was probably suffering more than any of the others. As a once-proud leader, his very heart and soul seemed to be impaled on those cold iron bars. Now, when his companions needed him more than ever before, there was nothing he could do. Sam's eyes, however, reflected outright fear and self-pity as he leapt against the bars until he wore himself out. Scruffy's feelings were those of helpless confusion. Unlike Sam, she just lay quietly at Butch's feet knowing that, but for her, the bull terrier would not have been there at all.

Afternoon was visiting time . . . a time when the

inmates did just about everything a dog could do to be noticed. They scaled each other's backs, buffeting and nipping one another out of the way, stretching to nudge any hand within reach or just to paw the ground outside. Some sat up and begged for hours on end. Others rolled over on their backs in a way they knew had once impressed their lost owners.

Occasionally, a cell door would creak open a few inches and all would surge forward like panic-stricken passengers on a sinking ship. The lucky one the kennelman let through would be carried off as the rest watched it go, burning with envy. Once it was out of sight they would then slump despondently to the ground until the next visitor approached. When one did, even an instant's hesitation was enough to start the mad scramble all over again.

Only the oldest dogs held back. For them, just anybody wouldn't do . . . though they still watched faces and listened to footsteps in case the right ones came along. Perhaps they felt it was too late to begin again with someone new.

The Wednesday dogs seemed the most desperate . . . almost as if they knew today was their last chance. It is difficult to understand how they could have known. But, as any kennelman will tell you, dogs do sense these things. Certainly Faith, Hope and Charity hollered louder and longer than they'd ever done before — and it paid off. Ten minutes before closing time the matron of a children's home adopted all three.

It was Wednesday afternoon and from the rumpus taking place inside the dog delivery van as it drove through the gates, you'd have thought it was returning with a herd of wild game from an African safari.

The driver leapt from his cab. 'For Pete's sake,' he bellowed across the yard, 'will someone come and give me a lift with this bunch? There's a bandy little cairn in here. It's wading into a great dane like a ferret and the rest are going berserk. I've never seen anything like it. It's not much bigger than a feather duster.'

George hurried over as dull thuds shuddered the big red van. When they unlocked the rear doors, the great dane bounded out, flattening the driver against a wall with paws like boxing gloves. An instant later the cairn tried to leap after it but bounced back against the van doors as the kennelman slammed them. 'It's ludicrous,' panted the driver as the great dane licked his face. 'Look at the size of this brute — yet it's frightened to death.' The other man led the dog to a Wednesday cell and returned to tackle the cairn.

Scruffy peered incredulously between the bars as they finally dragged it from the van and bundled it into a smaller cell on its own. It was Solo all right. And there wasn't the slightest doubt that the cross-eyed boxer now stumbling out of the van was dear old Hamlet. A moment later he was rubbing noses with Butch and Sam through the bars separating the Tuesday and Wednesday cells.

The kennelmen watched them. 'They seem to know each other,' smiled George. 'Look how friendly they are.' The other grunted. 'He's an ugly-looking customer, that boxer. I don't fancy his chances.'

'No, that's the trouble. No-one takes the ugly ones. Yet I'll bet he'd be a faithful old thing if only someone'd give him the chance. Look at the way that toffee-nosed bloodhound's weighing him up. It's a real snob that one. Mind you, it'll be out of here soon. It's owner's just been on the phone. She was hysterical with grief. She's sending her chauffeur to pick it up.'

That afternoon when the visitors came, Sam's heart fluttered as George opened the cell door and led him to the office. A man stood with his arms folded, watching Sam and humming to himself. The Alsatian whimpered appealingly, rolling over onto his back and pawing the air like he'd seen the other dogs do. The stranger scowled then lunged forward as if to strike Sam with the back of his hand. The dog cowered in fright and, when the man shook his fist in front of his nose, Same licked it all over. As the visitor stalked from the room the kennelman raised his eyes to the ceiling. 'You blithering idiot,' he groaned. 'That was the wrong routine altogether. He wanted a guard dog. I shudder to think what you'd do if you met a burglar. Hug him to death I suppose.'

One visitor seemed quite taken with Butch, but his wife tugged his sleeve. 'No, no, Henry,' she cried, 'not that one. I've read about those dogs. They're killers.' The man shook her off and knelt down, pushing his face to within an inch of Butch's. The bull terrier flicked the tip of the man's nose with his tongue. 'Doesn't look much like a killer to me, Doris.'

The woman clutched his shoulder. 'Come away Henry, do,' she wailed, 'it's liable to tear your throat out.' He rubbed Butch's shiny coat. 'You're barmy, Doris. I'll bet he's as gentle as a lamb.' His wife snorted impatiently. 'Anyway,' she persisted, 'that's really beside the point Henry. We're here for a miniature poodle. You promised that's what we'd have. You know how mother likes miniature poodles.' Her husband gave her a wry look. If what she'd said about bull terriers was really true, he couldn't think of a better dog to take back to his mother-in-law.

One or two people stopped to ruffle Scruffy's neck, but that was all. They just wrinkled their noses and said things like 'too scraggy . . .' or 'a bit ordinary . . .' or '. . . it's the wrong size.' George nearly collapsed when he overheard one woman point out to her friend that '. . . it wouldn't match the carpet.'

If ever a dog tried to incite compassion it was Hamlet. But the moment he fixed a passer-by with those cross-sighted, bloodshot eyes, they shuddered and hurried away. Solo, of course, did nothing whatsoever to endear himself to anyone.

The kennelmen did their best to find homes for the less alluring dogs but, as usual, it was the thoroughbreds that claimed attention. At the end of the day Butch and his gang were still there. So was Moses. George shook his head. 'Why the devil can't more people look into an animal's eyes instead of its pedigree?' His colleague shrugged. 'Don't know. But I certainly wish someone'd take that perishing cairn. It's already nipped two of the visitors.'

19

The long empty nights were the worst. During the day there was always the chance, however slim, that a visitor might put their foot in death's door. At night there was nothing but shadows. Nothing to do but wait and fret and sometimes dream in fitful trembling sleep. And now it was Monday . . . the day the Tuesday dogs would be making their final public appearance.

There were more visitors than usual. A short-sighted old lady actually stopped to talk to Hamlet. She didn't take him, of course. But it made him feel important.

Butch and Scruffy got a few friendly pats and a couple asked questions about the grief-stricken Sam. But nothing came of this either. Even Solo must have sensed how little time he had left. He didn't bite anyone all day.

It was shortly after lunch that two men stood outside the Tuesday cell chatting to the superintendent of the home. One had a box-like object which he kept holding against his eye. Every now and then it flashed like lightning, making the dogs blink. Scruffy found that, for a few moments afterwards, she couldn't see properly. It terrified Sam, who huddled in a corner until the men left. Before they did, one of them crouched down and inspected the metal disc on the bitch's collar — the one Joseph Tibbles had given her.

As the gates of the dogs' home grated shut for the evening, the kennelmen made their final round of the cells like prison warders. They stayed a while by the Tuesday cell stroking the animals in turn. 'Sorry chums,' sighed George. 'We tried our best. It's just the luck of the draw I suppose.' He unwrapped a parcel and gave each dog a few scraps of meat.

They came for Butch just before nine o'clock on Tuesday morning. Like Scruffy and Sam, he had been given his last meal half an hour before. None of them had eaten very much. The kennelmen had just taken Moses, who'd fought like the very devil. It was ludicrous really, considering his size. Sam had gone berserk too when he saw the terrier go, and Scruffy felt sick with fear.

Butch wouldn't make any trouble though. Not that he lacked the courage to fight for survival. He'd done that often enough — like the time he took on the bull mastiff in the park. But this was different. This time he knew he couldn't win. In any case he would go proudly, if only to give fortitude to the others.

When George unlatched the cell door, Scruffy thrust forward first and tried to bar the opening with her body, but the man eased her gently to one side allowing Butch to walk through.

Solo watched from solitary confinement and couldn't understand why his leader didn't tear the man apart. They'd have a fight and a half on their hands when they came for him, that was sure.

Scruffy pressed her face between the bars as Butch

trotted away and she whimpered softly when he glanced back for the last time before turning into the red-brick building at the far end of the yard.

As the green wooden door closed behind the bull terrier, the gang stared at it as though they'd all been hypnotised. None of them made a sound or moved a muscle as the seconds ticked by. They had seen so many other dogs go through there and never come out. Scruffy's head slid down the bars and suddenly she howled like a coyote . . .

As she did so, a bell started ringing in the superintendent's white stone house. It stopped and, a few seconds later, the man burst out and rushed across the yard. 'George, George . . .' he bellowed at the top of his voice, '. . . stop! Hold everything!' The door opened and George thrust his head out. 'What is it?' The other panted towards him. 'It's that skinny little bitch in the Tuesday cage.'

'Scruffy?'

'Yes.'

'Oh blimey — what's she done?'

'Only got herself all over the front page of this morning's Daily Mirror. That was a reporter on the phone . . . the one who called here yesterday. He says the switchboard at their head office is jammed with calls from people who want to give her a home.' He tossed George a coin. 'Here, pop down the road and get a copy of the paper. Let's see what the blazes it's all about.'

The gang watched the superintendent barge through the green door. When he reappeared, Scruffy went wild with delight. Butch was padding along at the man's heels. The next instant the bull terrier shot across the yard to the Tuesday cell, where he feverishly licked the bitch's face through the bars.

George came scurrying through the main gates waving a rolled up newspaper. 'Wait till you read this,' he wheezed, opening it out in front of the other man's face. Printed across the top of page one was the word 'SCRUFFY' in letters an inch and a half deep. Below was a huge picture of the sad-eyed little bitch staring out of the Tuesday cell.

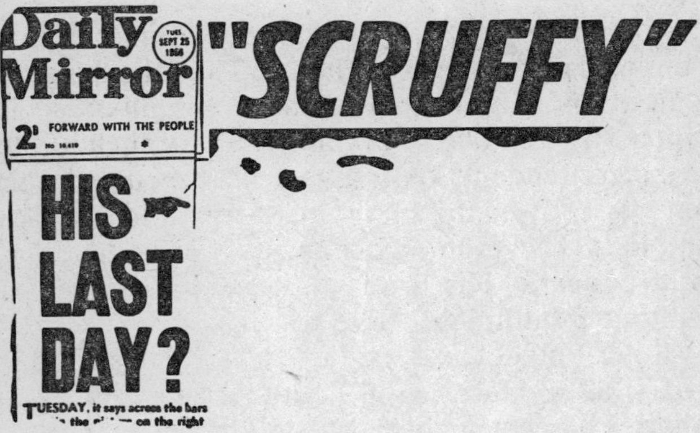
Daily Mirror

TUES SEPT 25 1956

2D FORWARD WITH THE PEOPLE

No 16,419

"SCRUFFY"

HIS LAST DAY?

TUESDAY, it says across the bars [illegible] on the right

'There's more,' puffed George. 'Turn to the middle pages.' Another bold headline screamed: 'SCRUFFY — THE DOG IN THE TUESDAY CAGE,' and there was a heart-rending appeal to the newspaper's millions of readers to save the dog from execution.

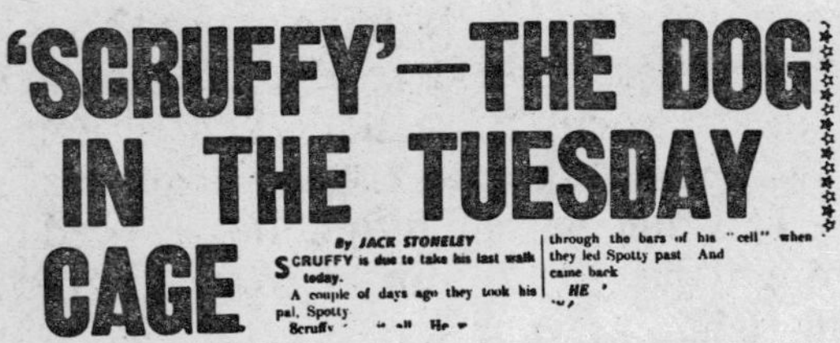
'SCRUFFY'—THE DOG IN THE TUESDAY CAGE

By JACK STONELEY

SCRUFFY is due to take his last walk today.

A couple of days ago they took his pal, Spotty

Scruffy [illegible] He [illegible]

through the bars of his "cell" when they led Spotty past And came back

HE [illegible]

The telephone rang again. The superintendent's wife popped her head through the window. 'The operator's just been on,' she cried. 'She says they've got about a dozen long-distance calls waiting to be put through. Shall I handle them?' Her husband stuffed the newspaper into his pocket. 'Yes love, thanks. Just take their names. Tell them we've plenty of other strays beside Scruffy. I'll take over in a few minutes.'

Soon there was a two-hour waiting list for incoming calls to the dogs' home. Then the telegrams began to pour in. They came from all over the country. 'Incredible . . . fantastic . . . unbelievable,' the superintendent kept saying as he ripped them open. '. . . Even the blooming Army and the Navy want her. The Home Secretary'll be demanding a reprieve next.' His wife put her hand over the telephone mouthpiece. 'I've just had a call from the Royal Air Force, too,' she hissed, 'they're asking for Scruffy as a mascot.' The little black and white mongrel, it seemed, had suddenly become the most wanted dog in Britain.

Long before visiting time a crowd began to gather outside the dogs' home. The superintendent mopped his brow. 'There'll be a stampede when we open those gates, George. Put the dog in my office until we decide what's to be done.' He turned to his wife: 'Leave the phone off the hook for a minute love, and make us a cup of tea. We're going to need one.'

The kennelman hurried to the Tuesday cell and clipped a lead to Scruffy's collar, but she rammed her front paws against the gate as Butch leapt snarling to her side. This time he would fight if they tried to take *her* through the green door. George grinned. 'All right, all right . . . your boyfriend can come too if it'll make you happy,' he said, leading the pair of them back to the office.

Here the superintendent weighed up Scruffy and sighed: 'Well, young lady, you've really started something. They're making more fuss of you than Liz Taylor.'

He looked through the window. The crowd outside was still growing. 'Reckon if I put you to sleep now, that lot out there would lynch me.' He glanced at the clock on the wall. 'Better let 'em in George. Bring the first half dozen in here and we'll decide who gets Scruffy. And tell the others that every dog in the place needs a home just as much as she does.' The kennelman carried out his instructions.

The next hour or so was chaotic. When visitors failed to find Scruffy they took the first reasonable-looking dog they saw, bustling each other aside to fondle the bewildered animals through the bars. Emotional women began snapping them up like special offers at a supermarket as children dragged their exhausted fathers from cell to cell. By two o'clock more than a hundred dogs had been claimed.

The kennelmen watched them being carried off — tails ticking like metronomes. 'It doesn't make sense,' muttered George. 'until a few hours ago nobody wanted to know any of 'em. Now you'd think they were all show dog champions. They're even after that wretched cairn.'

'I don't believe it George.'

'They are — look.'

Two women were haggling outside Solo's cell and the transformation in the little ruffian was quite incredible. He was actually licking their fingers.

'It's mine,' screeched one of the women.

'No it's not,' snapped the other, 'I saw it first.'

'Take your hands off it — see, it wants to come with me. You can tell.'

'No it doesn't . . . here boy, here boy — come to your Auntie Freda . . .' And on they went.

Meanwhile, the superintendent was considering who should get Scruffy from the group of people in his office. One of them — a blustery old ex-Army colonel — withdrew his claim the moment he spotted Butch. 'Aah,' he roared slapping the dog's brawny back, 'now this is what I call a real dog. Come here laddie, let's have a look at you.'

The bull terrier stood before him, rigid as a Coldstream Guard. The colonel beamed. 'look at those battle scars. He's got character — what! A dog after me own heart, this . . . all blood and guts . . . none of yer namby-pamby lap dogs. What a mascot he'd have made fer the old regiment, eh? Reminds me of my sergeant major. Lost him at Passchendaele y'know. Great chap that.' He paid the necessary fee and handed the dog's lead to a uniformed chauffeur standing to attention behind him. 'Here, Johnson — take my friend to the Rolls. I'll be along in a jiffy.'

Scruffy whined and rubbed her head against the bull terrier's throat. 'They're quite attached to each other,' explained the superintendent. 'They were brought in together.' The colonel hummed a military march and tapped the side of his fruity nose. 'Mm — I see,' he said at length. 'Here . . .' He whipped a card from the top pocket of his tweed jacket. 'When you've sorted out who gets Scruffy, give 'em this. Tell 'em she can come and stay with us whenever they like . . . got lots of ground . . . have the time of their lives — all right?'

'You're very kind, sir,' said the superintendent.

'Nonsense man, nonsense,' grunted the colonel. 'Got to keep the old soldier happy, haven't we? Every fighting man needs a good woman . . . only natural, eh? Same in the war.'

As for Scruffy, it was really she herself who selected her new owner by knocking him flat onto his back with her paws and licking his chubby cheeks. He was only four years old and his father had been the first person to telephone the dogs' home that morning. A few weeks before, the boy had seen his own dog killed by a milk float outside his home and had been inconsolable since. Now, as he flung his arms round Scruffy's neck and hugged her, the superintendent handed him the bitch's lead. 'It seems she's made up her own mind,' he smiled, '. . . I've learned never to argue with a female. Take care of her sonny — she's more famous than Rin-Tin-Tin.'

Outside, the other dogs were still being led or carried away by visitors. Sam was taken by a butcher who was already feeding him chunks of raw liver from a paper bag as the ecstatic Alsatian smothered the man's face with wet kisses — his tongue steaming like a fillet steak. Short of getting the owner of a stud kennel, Sam could not have made a better choice himself.

Solo had already gone off in the fur-coated arms of his triumphant 'Auntie Freda', who had finally outwitted the other woman — blissfully unaware of the carnage that lay ahead once the animal was introduced to her poodle-ridden neighbourhood.

At the end of the day the only member of the gang still unadopted was Hamlet, and his spirits sank to the concrete floor of his lonely Wednesday cell as he watched the others go. Even now, it seemed, nothing he did would endear him to anyone. George tried to console him. 'There's always tomorrow, old son,' he said unconvincingly. 'There's plenty of room here now. We'll give you a few extra days — how's that?'

And then — five minutes before the home closed — a man came hurrying across the yard towards them.

'Ah — there you are, you boozy old villain,' he cried. 'Someone told me I'd find you here.' Hamlet's backside did a shimmy that almost shook him off his feet. It was the landlord from the Prince of Denmark.

'You know each other then?' asked George.

'Know him — 'course I know him. He's one of my regulars. The place hasn't been the same without him.'

'You mean you'll take him?'

''Course I will. Don't know why I didn't do it a long time ago. Come on Hamlet — it's after opening time. I'll bet you could murder a meat pie and a pint.'

Wednesday's Daily Mirror summed up the remarkable way the public had rallied to Scruffy's aid. The following are actual excerpts from its report . . .

TUESDAY'S DOG IS WEDNESDAY'S JOY

By JACK STONELEY

Never before has one little lost mongrel had such an impact on a nation . . .

People travelled hundreds of miles to queue outside her cell marked 'Tuesday' at the home for lost dogs.

Forty-eight hours ago when the Daily Mirror found Scruffy staring through the bars of her cell nobody wanted her.

But from 9 a.m. yesterday officials at the dogs' home answered 100 phone calls an hour right through the day.

Even GPO girls waited among the long list of callers to the home to ask: 'How is Scruffy? Will she die?'

Five hundred appealing telegrams arrived from every part of Britain.

At the Daily Mirror offices more than 2,000 offers were made for Scruffy. (The total later reached a phenomenal 10,000).

One telegram came from Santa Margherita, Italy. 'Air-mail her,' pleaded a dog-lover, 'all expenses at my charge. Advise me for arrival.'

Even the Army, the RAF and the Navy asked for Scruffy. From the boys of 264 Squadron, Linton-On-Ouse, Yorkshire, came the wire: 'Offer home for Scruffy. Guaranteed best treatment.'

And from 'the boys' of 15 Mess, HMS Osprey, Portland, Dorset, came the signal: 'Save Scruffy — we will have her.'

From Catterick Army Camp, Yorkshire, came this message: 'We'll have her . . . letter following.'

Offers came from hospitals, schools, institutions. Some people even bought licences for Scruffy . . .

. . . The mountain of telegrams and the surge of telephone pleas reached fantastic proportions.

More than half of all calls into the Daily Mirror office were for Scruffy. And by the afternoon all lines to the dogs' home were jammed — mainly by incoming trunk calls.

Said an official: 'Never has there been anything like this before.'

Two hours after the home opened yesterday every dog was saved.

All those that could leave yesterday went. The rest had promises of homes.

Even the Post Office telegram boy who had delivered the piles of telegrams didn't leave without taking a stray dog.

And yesterday at dogs' homes all over Britain came offers of homes for strays . . .

It had, indeed, been the Day of the Lost Dogs.

George the kennelman read the report as he watched a fresh batch of strays being unloaded from the big red delivery van and shook his head sadly. 'Hard luck, fellas', he murmured, ' . . . you're just too late. You've missed the amnesty.'

EPILOGUE

Scruffy's story did not end on that extraordinary Tuesday afternoon at the dogs' home. Far from it.

Soon after this the Daily Mirror chose her for their coveted 'Dog of the Year' award and invited her to be guest of honour at a unique luncheon in the Louis Room of London's Cafe Royal. It was to inaugurate the now famous National Pets Club, and the high-class restaurant had seen nothing remotely like it before.

All kinds of creatures attended, including dogs, cats, rabbits, budgerigars, ponies, alligators, snakes, goats and monkeys. The eight-course meal ranged through sixty different items, like boiled bones, fish heads and iced buns, with special delicacies such as insect hors d'oeuvres and sauté of ants for the more exotic guests.

However, when the great day came, this headline appeared in the Mirror . . .

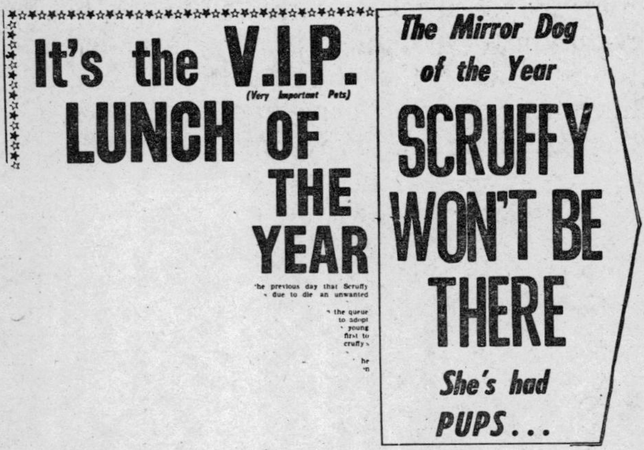
It's the V.I.P. (Very Important Pets) LUNCH OF THE YEAR

The Mirror Dog of the Year
SCRUFFY WON'T BE THERE
She's had PUPS...

'It's the V.I.P. (Very Important Pets)
Lunch of the Year.

SCRUFFY
WON'T Be
THERE.
She's had
PUPS . . .

'Scruffy, the most famous of all Mirror dogs, will have to cancel her biggest date of the year,' the report began, '. . . for the happiest of reasons.

'She has become a Mum . . .'

And yes — as you've no doubt guessed — every one had a streak of bull terrier in them!

It was, as Joseph P. Tibbles and William Shakespeare would surely have remarked, 'a case of All's Well That Ends Well.'

PUBLISHERS NOTE

The remarkable last-minute reprieve of a mongrel called Scruffy from the death cell of a home for strays is true. The author himself found her there and wrote the newspaper articles referred to in this book. The previous history of the Tuesday Dog, however, is fictitious — as are the human characters — though all the incidents described have happened to actual dogs and are based on brief Press reports of their exploits.

TARGET STORY BOOKS

Adventure

	Gordon Boshell			
113918	**THE BLACK MERCEDES**			60p
114043	**THE MILLION POUND RANSOM**			60p
117468	**THE MENDIP MONEY-MAKERS**			60p

Animal Stories

	Molly Burkett			
118502	**FOXES, OWLS AND ALL**	(NF)	(illus)	70p
111567	**THAT MAD, BAD BADGER . . .**	(NF)	(illus)	35p
	Constance Taber Colby			
109899	**A SKUNK IN THE FAMILY**	(NF)	(illus)	45p
	I. J. Edmonds			
20011X	**LASSIE: THE WILD MOUNTAIN TRAIL**			60p
	G. D. Griffiths			
113675	**ABANDONED!**		(illus)	50p
	David Gross			
117549	**THE BADGERS OF BADGER HILL**		(illus)	50p
	Michael Maguire			
118774	**MYLOR, THE MOST POWERFUL HORSE IN THE WORLD**		(illus)	60p
	Joyce Stranger			
11017X	**THE SECRET HERDS**		(illus)	45p
110099	**THE HARE AT DARK HOLLOW**		(illus)	40p

Mystery And Suspense

	Ruth M. Arthur			
111648	**THE AUTUMN GHOSTS**		(illus)	50p
111729	**THE CANDLEMAS MYSTERY**		(illus)	45p*
	Tim Dinsdale			
105915	**THE STORY OF THE LOCH NESS MONSTER**		(illus)	50p
	Leonard Gribble			
104285	**FAMOUS HISTORICAL MYSTERIES**	(NF)	(illus)	50p
	Alfred Hitchcock (Editor)			
117387	**ALFRED HITCHCOCK'S TALES OF TERROR AND SUSPENSE**			60p
	Mollie Hunter			
113756	**THE WALKING STONES**		(illus)	45p*
	Freya Littledale			
107357	**GHOSTS AND SPIRITS OF MANY LANDS**		(illus)	50p

†For sale in Britain and Ireland only.
***Not for sale in Canada.**
♦ Film & T.V. tie-ins.

TARGET STORY BOOKS

Fantasy And General Fiction

	Elisabeth Beresford		
101537	AWKWARD MAGIC	(illus)	60p
10479X	SEA-GREEN MAGIC	(illus)	60p
101618	TRAVELLING MAGIC	(illus)	60p
	Eileen Dunlop		
119142	ROBINSHEUGH	(illus)	60p
	Maria Gripe		
112288	THE GLASSBLOWER'S CHILDREN	(illus)	45p
	Joyce Nicholson		
117891	FREEDOM FOR PRISCILLA		70p
	Hilary Seton		
106989	THE HUMBLES	(illus)	50p
109112	THE NOEL STREATFEILD CHRISTMAS HOLIDAY BOOK	(illus)	60p
109031	THE NOEL STREATFEILD EASTER HOLIDAY BOOK	(illus)	60p
105249	THE NOEL STREATFEILD SUMMER HOLIDAY BOOK	(illus)	50p

Humour

	Eleanor Estes		
107519	THE WITCH FAMILY	(illus)	50p
	Felice Holman		
11762X	THE WITCH ON THE CORNER	(illus)	50p
	Spike Milligan		
105672	BADJELLY THE WITCH	(illus)	60p
109546	DIP THE PUPPY	(illus)	60p
	Christine Nostlinger		
107438	THE CUCUMBER KING	(illus)	45p
	Mary Rogers		
119223	A BILLION FOR BORIS		60p

0426 Film And TV Tie-ins

	Kathleen N. Daly		
200187	RAGGEDY ANN AND ANDY	(Colour illus)	75p ◆*
	John Ryder Hall		
11826X	SINBAD AND THE EYE OF THE TIGER		70p* ◆
	John Lucarotti		
11535X	OPERATION PATCH		45p
	Pat Sandys		
119495	THE PAPER LADS		60p ◆
	Alison Thomas		
115511	BENJI		40p

† For sale in Britain and Ireland only.
* Not for sale in Canada.
◆ Film & T.V. tie-ins.

TARGET STORY BOOKS

'Doctor Who'

0426			
200098	Terrance Dicks **DOCTOR WHO AND THE HORROR OF FANG ROCK**		60p
108663	Brian Hayles **DOCTOR WHO AND THE ICE WARRIORS**		60p
110412	Terrance Dicks **DOCTOR WHO AND THE LOCH NESS MONSTER**		60p
118936	Philip Hinchcliffe **DOCTOR WHO AND THE MASQUE OF MANDRAGORA**		60p
116909	Terrance Dicks **DOCTOR WHO AND THE MUTANTS**		60p
116828	Terrance Dicks **DOCTOR WHO AND THE PLANET OF EVIL**		60p
116666	Terrance Dicks **DOCTOR WHO AND THE PYRAMIDS OF MARS**		60p
11308X	Malcolm Hulke **DOCTOR WHO AND THE SEA-DEVILS**	(illus)	40p
116585	Philip Hinchcliffe **DOCTOR WHO AND THE SEEDS OF DOOM**		50p
110331	Malcolm Hulke **DOCTOR WHO AND THE SPACE WAR**		60p
119738	Terrance Dicks **DOCTOR WHO AND THE TALONS OF WENG-CHIANG**		60p
110846	Terrance Dicks **DOCTOR WHO AND THE WEB OF FEAR**		60p
113241	Bill Strutton **DOCTOR WHO AND THE ZARBI**	(illus)	60p
114477	Terrance Dicks **THE DOCTOR WHO MONSTER BOOK**	(illus)	50p
200012	**THE SECOND DOCTOR WHO MONSTER BOOK**	(Colour illus)	70p
118421	Terrance Dicks **THE DOCTOR WHO DINOSAUR BOOK**		75p
116151	Terrance Dicks and Malcolm Hulke **THE MAKING OF DOCTOR WHO**		60p

†For sale in Britain and Ireland only.
*Not for sale in Canada.
♦ Film & T.V. tie-ins.

TARGET STORY BOOKS

'Doctor Who'

200020	DOCTOR WHO DISCOVERS PREHISTORIC ANIMALS	(NF)	(illus)	75p
200039	DOCTOR WHO DISCOVERS SPACE TRAVEL	(NF)	(illus)	75p
200047	DOCTOR WHO DISCOVERS STRANGE AND MYSTERIOUS CREATURES	(NF)	(illus)	75p
20008X	DOCTOR WHO DISCOVERS THE STORY OF EARLY MAN	(NF)	(illus)	75p
200136	DOCTOR WHO DISCOVERS THE CONQUERORS	(NF)	(illus)	75p
116313	Ian Marter DOCTOR WHO AND THE ARK IN SPACE			50p
116747	Terrance Dicks DOCTOR WHO AND THE BRAIN OF MORBIUS			50p*
110250	Terrance Dicks DOCTOR WHO AND THE CARNIVAL OF MONSTERS			50p
11471X	Malcolm Hulke DOCTOR WHO AND THE CAVE MONSTERS			60p
117034	Terrance Dicks DOCTOR WHO AND THE CLAWS OF AXOS			50p*
113160	David Whitaker DOCTOR WHO AND THE CRUSADERS		(illus)	60p
114981	Brian Hayles DOCTOR WHO AND THE CURSE OF PELADON			60p
114639	Gerry Davis DOCTOR WHO AND THE CYBERMEN			60p
113322	Barry Letts DOCTOR WHO AND THE DAEMONS		(illus)	40p
101103	David Whitaker DOCTOR WHO AND THE DALEKS			60p
11244X	Terrance Dicks DOCTOR WHO AND THE DALEK INVASION OF EARTH			60p
119657	Terrance Dicks DOCTOR WHO AND THE DEADLY ASSASSIN			60p
200063	Terrance Dicks DOCTOR WHO AND THE FACE OF EVIL			60p
112601	Terrance Dicks DOCTOR WHO AND THE GENESIS OF THE DALEKS			60p

†For sale in Britain and Ireland only.
*Not for sale in Canada.
♦ Film & T.V. tie-ins.